NEW TRAPS IN THE CHESS OPENING

NEW TRAPS
IN THE
CHESS OPENING

AL HOROWITZ

AN
ARC
BOOK
ARCO PUBLISHING COMPANY, INC.
219 Park Avenue South, New York, N.Y. 10003

An ARC Book
Published by ARCO Publishing Company, Inc.
219 Park Avenue South, New York, N.Y. 10003

Third Printing, 1973

Library of Congress Catalog Card Number 64-17715
ISBN 0-668-02191-8

Printed in the United States of America

INTRODUCTION

THIS BOOK IS A COLLECTION of 175 chess traps, most of which evolve from variations of modern openings. Included also are a number of older traps which are required knowledge for every aspiring chessplayer.

Many of the selections were discovered by examining thousands of games from tournaments throughout the world; others were submitted by researchers. The field has by no means been exhausted. We have tried only to cull the best of the available harvest. Many traps in the middle and endgame, in fact, are beyond the scope of this work.

To begin with, let us define a trap by what it is *not*. Every combination, unexpected turn or deviation from standard practice in the opening is not necessarily a trap. These may be merely optional continuations, of which there are so many in chess.

A trap is a sly stratagem with a baited offer, tangible or intangible, the acceptance of which triggers a punitive combination. The offer may take the form of material, time, space, or anything which creates the impression that it is either an outright blunder or a forced play in response to some "mighty fine" moves of the adversary. It must be plausible and deceptive, leaving the victim unaware of its true significance until he is stung beyond repair.

Here is a two-move (!) game which is not a trap: 1 P–KB4, P–K3; 2 P–KN4, Q–R5 mate. There is nothing baited in Black's first move to induce White's foolish second move. Hence, White has stepped into a pitfall of his own design, and from Black's point of view, it is a windfall. The idea embodied in this example, on the other hand, is pertinent to many a trap abounding in this work.

Here is an elementary trap: 1 P–K4, P–K4; 2 N–KB3, N–QB3; 3 B–B4, N–Q5. The bait is Black's last move; it leaves the King Pawn unguarded. It holds out to White prospects of even greater gain. For after he captures the King Pawn, he is doubly threatening Black's vulnerable King Bishop Pawn. Perhaps White should inquire as to the meaning of Black's generosity. Then, perhaps, he might discern the diabolical idea. But greed is an overpowering emotion and leaves little

Introduction

time for questions. So White plays 4 NxP. Black replies 4 ... Q–N4, the stinger, and White is lost. The continuation might be 5 NxBP, QxP; 6 R–B1, QxKP†; 7 B–K2, N–B6 checkmate.

Here is a more sophisticated trap based on tactics, one that includes bait which accelerates the win:

1 P–Q4, P–Q4; 2 P–QB4, P–K4 (this is Albin's Counter Gambit. A gambit, per se, is not a trap). 3 PxKP, P–Q5; 4 P–K3?, B–N5†; 5 B–Q2, PxP. Now White can play 6 PxP. Then Black will recover his Pawn eventually and actually enjoy the better position. But White can capture a whole piece, apparently for nothing. Why not? Quickly he attributes this absurdity to a *fingerfehler* ("finger-slip") on the part of Black. And so he plays 6 BxB. There follows 6 ... PxP†; 7 K–K2, PxN/N† and White is lost. White failed to foresee this last underpromotion, and could not control his greed.

Even more sophisticated is the purely positional trap conceived by the former World Champion, Jose Raoul Capablanca, as Black against the eccentric modernist, Savielly Tartakover. It is from the famous tournament held in New York, 1924:

1 P–K4, P–K4; 2 P–KB4, PxP; 3 B–K2. This, the Little Bishop's Gambit, was Tartakover's pet opening, which he played with success against Alekhine and Bogolubov. There followed 3 ... P–Q4; 4 PxP, N–KB3; 5 P–B4, P–B3; 6 P–Q4, B–N5†; 7 K–B1, PxP; 8 BxP, PxP. With a gesture of surprise and joy, thinking that the mighty Capablanca had blundered, Tartakover continued with 9 BxN. He now expected ... RxB, after which he would play 10 Q–R4†, winning a piece. Lo and behold, Capablanca played instead 9 ... N–Q4. And Tartakover's position burst at the seams. The threat was 10 ... N–K6†, which assured the recovery of the piece in a position where White had forfeited castling and shattered his Pawn structure.

Thus we see that traps may have varying degrees of complexity; they range from the blatant to the subtle. Although this book will not provide a magic key to the mastery of traps, it contains a wide range of "trappy" ideas, themes and motifs, familiarity with which is essential for the serious chessplayer. A knowledge of these traps will also give the

Introduction

casual or "friendly game" player a wide edge over opponents who are unfamiliar with these stratagems.

Finally, it must be remembered that the loser in each of these traps violates one or more of the basic chess principles, and in each case the punishment for this violation is clear and succinct.

By studying traps, one becomes a better all-around chess-player in two ways: by learning how to avoid violations of strategic and tactical principles, and by acquiring the ability to take advantage of mistakes when they are made by one's opponents.

There is a type of trap which has its infinite variations and countless disciples. For good and sufficient reason, it is not included in this collection. This is the "sour face" or "agitated agony" snare, known as the "coffee house." This ploy may be employed in a variety of positional situations, and works like this: You want to bait your opponent by offering him a Pawn or a piece. If he accepts, you have a winning game. Your adversary, however, is cautious. If you make your baited move in the usual deadpan manner, he will analyze it carefully. So you go into your act. Immediately after your hand has left the bait, your features contort, your cheeks flush and a half-suppressed exclamation of despair escapes from your mouth. Your opponent is sure you've blundered, or had a finger-slip. He grabs the piece, and you mate him in four.

Whether to employ this ruse must be left up to each chess-player's sense of ethics; we include the "coffee house" here only because it is strategy which must be included in any treatise which attempts to treat traps comprehensively!

THE FOLLOWING SYMBOLS ARE USED THROUGHOUT THIS BOOK:

   ! = Strong move
   !! = Exceptionally brilliant move
   ? = Weak move, or superior alternative has been overlooked
   !? = Spectacular move with a flaw
   ?! = Questionable move, but creates problems and complications
   † = Check, discovered check, double check

Contents

Alekhine's Defense

	WHITE	BLACK
1	P-K4	N-KB3
2	P-K5	N-Q4
3	N-KB3	P-Q3
4	P-Q4	B-N5
5	B-K2	PxP
6	NxP	BxB
7	QxB	N-N3
8	O-O	QxP?[1]
	see diagram	
9	R-Q1	Q-KR5[2]
10	B-N5!	QxB[3]
11	R-Q8†[4]	....

Black loses his Queen

WHITE TO PLAY

"Take first and look later" is Black's way. But retribution is stiff.

---

[1] A grave error in judgment. Black should play 8 ... QN-Q2 with a satisfactory game.

[2] Other Queen moves are worse, e.g. 9 ... Q-B4; 10 P-QN4, QxNP; 11 Q-B3, QN-Q2 (if 11 ... P-KB3; 12 Q-R5†, P-N3; 13 NxP, PxN; 14 QxP mate) 12 QxP†, K-Q1; 13 Q-K6 threatening 14 RxN† and 14 NxN as well as 14 N-B7†. If 9 ... Q-QR5 or 9 ... Q-QN5; 10 Q-B3 wins.

[3] Again forced, for if 10 ... Q-QR5 or 10 ... Q-QN5, 11 Q-B3 is still lethal.

[4] After 11 ... KxR; 12 NxP† and 13 NxQ, White has won the Queen for Rook and Bishop. White should win easily since Black's King and White squares are still vulnerable.

2 *Alekhine's Defense*

	WHITE	BLACK
1	P-K4	N-KB3
2	P-K5	N-Q4
3	P-QB4	N-N3
4	P-B5	N-Q4
5	B-B4	P-K3
6	N-QB3	NxN
7	QPxN	BxP
8	Q-N4	B-B1[1]
	see diagram	
9	B-KN5	B-K2[2]
10	BxB	QxB
11	QxNP	Q-B1
12	Q-B6	R-N1
13	B-Q3	Q-N2
14	N-B3	P-Q3[3]
15	O-O-O	QxQ
16	PxQ	RxP[4]
17	KR-N1	RxBP[5]
18	R-N8†	K-Q2
19	N-K5†	PxN
20	B-N5	....

Black has been checkmated

WHITE TO PLAY

Black should have defended his Knight Pawn by advancing it or moving his King. Either way would create a small weakness. Now his Pawn structure seems sound. Is it?

---

[1] Better is 8 ... K-B1.

[2] And not 9 ... P-KB3?; 10 PxP, PxP; 11 Q-R5†, K-K2; 12 BxP†, KxB; 13 Q-R4† winning the Queen.

[3] 14 ... QxP? loses to 15 R-KN1.

[4] A mistake. Black's first concern should be for the Pawn at KB6, and therefore 16 ... N-Q2 should be played, or possibly 16 ... P-KR3 followed by 17 QN-Q2. The open King Knight file gives White's Rook too much activity.

[5] This allows a pretty mate, but Black was already quite lost, e.g. 17 ... RxR, 18 RxR, K-B1; 19 BxP, or 17 ... RxR; 18 RxR, N-Q2; 19 R-N8†, N-B1; 20 N-N5, or here 17 ... RxR; 18 RxR, K-Q2; 19 R-N7 wins easily.

Benoni Defense

	WHITE	BLACK
1	P-Q4	N-KB3
2	P-QB4	P-B4
3	P-Q5	P-K3
4	N-QB3	PxP
5	PxP	P-Q3
6	P-K4	P-KN3
7	P-B4[1]	B-N2
8	P-K5	KN-Q2?[2]
	see diagram	
9	N-K4!	PxP
10	N-Q6†	K-B1
11	N-B3[3]	

WHITE TO PLAY

White has overextended his Pawn phalanx. Does he have compensation? That is the question.

White has great positional superiority

---

[1] The introduction to a novel but speculative attacking line.

[2] Black would do better to exchange the center Pawns before retreating the Knight. After 8 ... PxP; 9 PxP, KN-Q2, the situation would be decidedly unclear. After the next move, Black's chances to defend successfully are negligible.

[3] Black will have a very difficult time developing his game. 11 ... P-K5 is met by 12 N-KN5 and 11 ... PxP, eventually giving White the KB file to work on, is not attractive.

Bishop's Gambit

	WHITE	BLACK
1	P-K4	P-K4
2	B-B4	N-KB3
3	N-QB3	NxP
4	BxP†[1]	KxB
5	NxN	N-B3?[2]
6	Q-B3†	K-N1?[3]
	see diagram	
7	N-N5![4]	. . . .

Black will be checkmated or lose his Queen

WHITE TO PLAY

Black's last move is normal in most instances. But not here! Why?

---

[1] Tricky, but not White's best, which is 4 Q–R5.

[2] 5 . . . P–Q4 gives Black much the better game with his two Bishops and broad center, e.g. 5 . . . P–Q4; 6 Q–B3†, K–N1; 7 N–N5!?, Q–Q2! and now Black can develop very quickly and powerfully in a few moves.

[3] A blunder. Black still has an adequate position with 6 . . . K–K1.

[4] There is no defense, as all Queen moves are met by 8 Q–Q5†, and White otherwise will mate at KB7 with his Queen.

Blackmar Gambit

	WHITE	BLACK
1	P-Q4	P-Q4
2	P-K4	PxP
3	N-QB3	N-KB3[1]
4	P-B3	PxP
5	QxP!	QxP[2]
6	B-K3	Q-QN5
7	O-O-O	B-N5?[3]
	see diagram	
8	N-N5!	P-K4[4]
9	NxP†	K-K2
10	QxP![5]	. . . .

White has a winning attack

WHITE TO PLAY
Behind in development, Black ought to consolidate. But he is greedy.

[1] 3 . . . P–K4 is a simple and effective method of equalizing.

[2] Black is courting danger. Development should be the order of the day.

[3] And this finally loses. Black should play 7 . . . P-QB3 with fair chances of defending and eventually utilizing his material advantage.

[4] White's twin threats of 9 NxP mate and 9 QxNP cannot satisfactorily be met.

[5] For if 10 . . . QxQ; 11 B–B5 mate. Black's cause is hopeless, since White threatens 11 QxQ mate, or if 10 . . . P–QR4; 11 QxQ†, PxQ; 12 B–B5 mate.

6

	WHITE	BLACK
1	P-Q4	N-KB3
2	P-QB4	P-K4
3	PxP	N-N5
4	P-K4	NxKP
5	P-B4	N-N3
6	B-K3	N-B3
7	N-KB3	B-N5†
8	QN-Q2	Q-K2
9	B-Q3	O-O
10	O-O?[1]	B-B4![2]

see diagram

BLACK TO PLAY

A clever sortie exploits White's correct-looking but faulty last move. Black nets a big Pawn.

Black wins material

---

[1] This is careless and loses a Pawn. White should play 10 Q–K2 with the option of castling on either wing.

[2] Now if 11 BxB, QxB† and 12 . . . NxP, and if 11 Q–K1 or 11 Q–K2, the answer is still 11 . . . NxP. Black has won a Pawn with a good position.

Budapest Defense

WHITE	BLACK
1 P-Q4	N-KB3
2 P-QB4	P-K4
3 PxP	N-K5
4 P-QR3	P-Q3
5 N-KB3	N-QB3
6 PxP[1]	BxP
7 P-KN3?[2]	....

see diagram

7	NxBP
8 KxN[3]	BxP†[4]

White will lose his Queen

BLACK TO PLAY

A Pawn plus is not an automatic win. Circumspection will nurse it along. But White here was oblivious of the veiled but imminent threat.

[1] 6 Q-B2 is better.
[2] 7 QN-Q2 striving for exchanges was indicated, though Black's attacking chances are still good.
[3] 8 Q-B2, NxR; 9 B-N2, NxP; 10 PxN, BxP† and Black has an easy win.
[4] Black wins the Queen for two pieces.

8   *Budapest Defense*

	WHITE	BLACK
1	P-Q4	N-KB3
2	P-QB4	P-K4
3	PxP	N-K5
4	N-KB3	N-QB3
5	P-QR3	P-Q3
6	P-K3[1]	B-B4
7	PxP	BxP
8	B-K2	Q-B3
9	N-Q4?[2]	. . . .

see diagram

9	. . . .	NxP!
10	KxN[3]	B-B7†
11	N-B3	BxQ
12	RxB	N-K4
13	N-Q2	N-N5†
14	K-N1	BxP†

**Black wins decisive
material**

BLACK TO PLAY

*Beware the discovered check,
and observe the vulnerable
King Bishop Pawn. White is
remiss.*

---

[1] Too passive. White should play 6 Q–B2 and if 6 . . . B–B4; 7 N–QB3,
N–N6; 8 P–K4! or 7 . . . NxBP; 8 QxB with the better chances. Now
Black gets a fine attack.

[2] A blunder, losing immediately. However, after 9 O–O, O–O–O (threatening 10 . . . BxP† winning the Queen) Black is ready for . . . Q–R3
and a King-side storm: . . . P–KN4–N5, etc.

[3] If the Queen moves, 10 . . . NxR is equally bad for White. He can
offer no further resistance.

Caro-Kann Defense

	WHITE	BLACK
1	P-K4	P-QB3
2	P-Q4	P-Q4
3	N-QB3	PxP
4	NxP	N-B3
5	NxN†	KPxN[1]
6	B-QB4	B-K2
7	Q-R5	O-O
8	N-K2	P-KN3[2]
9	Q-B3	N-Q2?
10	B-KR6	R-K1[3]
	see diagram	
11	BxP†[4]	....

**White wins decisive
material**

WHITE TO PLAY

*Again, the guarded King
Bishop Pawn is vulnerable.
Here, the King is the butt.*

---

[1] Although this recapture affords Black free play for his minor pieces, he is left with a lasting disadvantage in the endgame. The White Pawn majority on the Queen's wing could easily prove decisive. Also, White's attacking chances are not to be underestimated, as this game demonstrates.

[2] 9 ... N-Q2 followed by 10 ... N-N3 is preferable to this weakening.

[3] Black's last chance was 10 ... Q-R4†, though White should maintain a positional advantage.

[4] 11 ... KxB is met by 12 Q-N3 mate, so White wins the exchange and a Pawn.

10 *Caro-Kann Defense*

	WHITE	BLACK
1	P-K4	P-QB3
2	P-Q4	P-Q4
3	N-QB3	PxP
4	NxP	N-B3
5	N-N3[1]	P-KR4
6	B-KN5[2]	P-R5
7	BxN[3]	PxN
8	B-K5[4]	RxP
9	RxR	....
	see diagram	
9	....	Q-R4†
10	P-B3	QxB†
11	PxQ	PxR[5]

BLACK TO PLAY

A clever combination promotes a mite of a Pawn.

Black wins decisive material

---

[1] 5 NxN† is preferable and maintains the initiative and the preferable Pawn structure for White.

[2] And this is very weak. Better would be 6 Q-Q3 or 6 P-KR4.

[3] The unpleasant 7 QN-K2 is forced to avoid material loss.

[4] In order to guard the KR2 square. Black threatened 8 . . . RxP 9 RxR, PxR and the Pawn must Queen.

[5] White cannot stop the Pawn from Queening, and Black will emerge a piece ahead.

Caro-Kann Defense

	WHITE	BLACK
1	P-K4	P-QB3
2	P-Q4	P-Q4
3	N-QB3	PxP
4	NxP	N-B3
5	Q-Q3[1]	P-K4?[2]
6	PxP	Q-R4†
7	B-Q2	QxKP
	see diagram	
8	O-O-O!	NxN?[3]
9	Q-Q8†	KxQ
10	B-N5†	. . . .[4]

White mates next move

WHITE TO PLAY
*White's Knight is in peril, and
White conjures up a fabulous
method of winning.*

---

[1] 5 NxN† is the usual move here and gives White some advantage.

[2] This opening up of the game is very risky. Preferable was 5 . . . NxN
6 QxN, N–Q2 followed by 7 . . . N–B3 with an easy game for Black.

[3] If 8 . . . QxR; 9 R–K1 wins the Queen, although that is preferable to
the move actually played. Black's best chance is 8 . . . B–K2, and he
has some hope of defending successfully.

[4] Now if 10 . . . K–K1; 11 R–Q8 is mate, or if 10 . . . K–B2; 11 B–Q8
is also mate.

Caro-Kann Defense

	WHITE	BLACK
1	P-K4	P-QB3
2	P-Q4	P-Q4
3	N-QB3	PxP
4	NxP	B-B4
5	N-N3	B-N3
6	N-B3	N-Q2
7	P-KR4	P-KR3
8	P-R5	B-R2
9	B-Q3	BxB
10	QxB	KN-B3
11	O-O	Q-B2
12	R-K1	P-K3
13	N-K5	B-K2?[1]

WHITE TO PLAY

The vulnerability of the King Bishop Pawn permits a powerful and decisive incursion.

	see diagram	
14	NxKBP	KxN
15	Q-N6†	K-N1[2]
16	N-B5	PxN[3]
17	RxB	R-R2
18	BxP	NxP[4]
19	Q-B7†	....[5]

White mates in three

[1] 13 ... NxN followed by 14 ... N-Q2 and 15 ... O-O-O was indicated.
[2] 15 ... K-B1; 16 RxP, R-K1; 17 N-B5, R-R2 (17 ... R-KN1; 18 NxNP) 18 NxNP!, RxN; 19 BxP is no better for Black.
[3] If 16 ... B-B1, simply 17 RxP and White has a ferocious attack. The Black KRP is indefensible and 18 R-K7 is also threatened.
[4] The KNP must be defended.
[5] 19 ... K-R1; 20 R-K8†, etc.

Caro-Kann Defense 13

	WHITE	BLACK
1	P-K4	P-QB3
2	P-Q4	P-Q4
3	N-QB3	PxP
4	NxP	B-B4
5	N-N3	B-N3
6	N-R3	P-KR3[1]
7	N-B4	B-R2
8	B-B4	P-K3
9	O-O	N-B3
10	R-K1	B-K2
11	Q-K2	N-Q4[2]
12	N/3-R5	O-O
13	BxN	BPxB
	see diagram	
14	NxNP	KxN
15	Q-K5†	K-N1[3]
16	N-R5	P-B3
17	QxP†	R-B2
18	BxP	Q-Q2[4]
19	NxP†	BxN
20	Q-K8†	....

Black cannot avoid checkmate

WHITE TO PLAY

Black's 6 . . . P-KR3 has cost him time later on, just enough for White to pierce the Black monarch's shelter.

[1] An unnecessary and time-consuming weakening.
[2] If 11 . . . QxP; 12 NxP! leads to a winning attack for White.
[3] If 15 . . . P-B3, 16 NxP†, K-R1 (or 16 K-N1 17 Q-N3†); 17 Q-N3, R-N1; 18 NxQ, RxQ; 19 RPxR, BxN; 20 R-K8†, and if 15 . . . B-B3; 16 N-R5†, K-N3; 17 NxB, QxN (or 17 . . . N-B3; 18 Q-R5†, KxN; 19 QxP†, K-K2; 20 QxB, or 19 . . . B-N3; 20 B-N5†) 18 Q-N3†, K-R4; 19 Q-R3†, Q-R5 (or 19 . . . K-N3; 20 QxP†, K-B4; 21 R-K5†) 20 P-N4† wins the Queen.
[4] The threat was 19 Q-N4† winning.

	WHITE	BLACK
1	P-K4	P-Q4
2	PxP	QxP
3	N-QB3	Q-QR4
4	P-Q4	N-KB3
5	N-B3	B-N5
6	P-KR3	B-R4[1]
7	P-KN4	B-N3
8	N-K5	P-QB3[2]
9	N-B4	Q-B2
10	Q-B3	BxP?[3]

see diagram

WHITE TO PLAY

A Pawn is a Pawn, and only an expert can tell when it's tainted. Here the Pawn-snatcher is punished quickly.

11	B-B4	Q-Q1
12	Q-K2!	B-N3[4]
13	N-Q6†	K-Q2
14	NxNP[5]	....

White has a winning attack

---

[1] 6 ... BxN; 7 QxB, P-B3, yielding the advantage of the two Bishops but maintaining a sound position, was more circumspect.

[2] Necessary to create a flight square for the Queen.

[3] Too greedy. Black should play 10 ... P-K3, though White has a clear advantage after 11 B-B4.

[4] Forced, for if 12 ... QxP; 13 B-K3 (or 13 B-K5 or 13 BxN) and White's extra piece assures an easy win.

[5] Black's position is in tatters. A typical variation might be 14 ... Q-N3; 15 N-R4, Q-N5† (15 ... QxN; 16 N-B5† wins the Queen) 16 B-Q2, QxQP; 17 O-O-O and Black is defenseless against the multiple threats against the King and the Queen.

Center Counter Game

	WHITE	BLACK
1	P-K4	P-Q4
2	PxP	QxP
3	N-QB3	Q-QR4
4	P-Q4	P-K4
5	PxP[1]	B-QN5
6	B-Q2[2]	N-QB3
7	P-QR3[3]	N-Q5[4]
8	PxB?[5]	....

see diagram

| 8 | .... | QxR |
| 9 | QxQ | NxP†[6] |

Black wins material

BLACK TO PLAY

The Bishop capture is crass, and Black shows its fallacy.

---

[1] 5 N-B3 is better calculated to maintain the White advantage.

[2] Here again 6 N-B3 is preferable.

[3] Hoping to force Black to a decision.

[4] Black prefers to speculate rather than to acquiesce to the easy draw which would result after 7 ... QxP†; 8 Q-K2. He also sets a trap.

[5] The decisive mistake. 8 P-KB4 and if 8 ... B-KB4; 9 R-QB1 should have been played, and Black's compensation for the Pawn is somewhat nebulous.

[6] Black is the Exchange ahead and should win, as his Knight will have no difficulty in escaping.

	WHITE	BLACK
1	P-K4	P-Q4
2	PxP	QxP
3	N-QB3	Q-QR4
4	N-B3	B-N5
5	P-KR3	BxN
6	QxB	N-QB3?[1]
7	B-N5	Q-N3[2]
	see diagram	
8	N-Q5	Q-R4[3]
9	P-QN4[4]	....

Black's Queen is lost

WHITE TO PLAY

*Undoubtedly, Black plays the
defense just to be different.
He loses just the same.*

---

[1] Black should play 6 ... P–QB3 here with only a minimal positional
disadvantage.

[2] Otherwise 8 BxN† wins.

[3] If 8 ... QxB; 9 NxP† wins the Queen, and if 8 ... Q–B4; 9 P–Q4!
and if 9 ... QxQP; 10 BxN†, PxB; 11 NxP†, or 9 QxBP, NxP†, or
finally 9 ... Q–Q3; 10 B–KB4, P–K4; 11 BxP and 12 NxP†.

[4] Black's Queen is lost, for if 9 ... QxB; 10 NxP†.

Center Counter Game 17

	WHITE	BLACK
1	P-K4	P-Q4
2	PxP	QxP
3	N-QB3	Q-Q1[1]
4	P-Q4	N-QB3[2]
5	N-B3	B-N5
6	P-Q5	N-K4[3]
	see diagram	
7	NxN	BxQ
8	B-N5†	P-B3
9	PxP	P-QR3[4]
10	P-B7†	PxB
11	PxQ/Q†	RxQ
12	NxB[5]	....

White has won decisive material

WHITE TO PLAY

The illusory pin plays havoc with Black's plan. Bent on development, Black fails to see the denouement.

[1] 3 ... Q–QR4 followed by an early ... P–QB3 is more usual for Black.
[2] And this is dubious, as the White Queen Pawn may advance with gain of tempo.
[3] Black overlooks the Queen sacrifice. The Knight had to retreat to N1.
[4] Black is helpless. If here 9 ... Q–B2; 10 PxP†, K–Q1; 11 NxP mate.
[5] And White, a piece ahead, can look forward to an easy victory.

18 *Center Counter Game*

	WHITE	BLACK
1	P-K4	P-Q4
2	PxP	N-KB3
3	N-QB3	NxP
4	B-B4	N-N3
5	B-N3	N-B3
6	N-B3	P-K4
7	P-Q3	B-KN5
8	P-KR3	B-R4?[1]
	see diagram	
9	NxP	BxQ
10	BxP†	K-K2
11	B-N5†	K-Q3
12	N-K4†	KxN
13	P-B4†	K-Q5[2]
14	RxB	K-K6[3]
15	O-O!	N-Q5
16	QR-K1†	N-K7†
17	RxN†	KxR[4]
18	B-R5†	K-K6
19	R-B3†	K-Q5
20	B-B7	. . . .[5]

Black cannot avoid checkmate

WHITE TO PLAY

When is a pin not a pin? Here is another case in point. White wins a Pawn or checkmates.

---

[1] Missing a surprising combination. 8 . . . BxN was necessary.

[2] If 13 . . . K-B4; 14 N-N3 mate.

[3] Black is helpless. Among other things White was threatening 15 K-K2 and 16 P-B3 mate.

[4] If 17 . . . K-Q5; 18 R-Q1 and 19 P-B3† follows.

[5] Again 21 P-B3† is curtains. A pleasing King-hunt!

Catalan Opening

	WHITE	BLACK
1	P-Q4	N-KB3
2	P-QB4	P-K3
3	N-KB3	P-Q4
4	P-KN3	PxP
5	QN-Q2	P-B4
6	PxP	BxP
7	B-N2?	....
	see diagram	
7	....	BxP†
8	KxB	N-N5†
9	K-K1	N-K6[1]

White will lose his Queen

BLACK TO PLAY
Again, the vulnerable King Bishop Pawn is the target, and it leads to the King or Queen.

---

[1] Black wins the Queen. If 10 Q–R4†, Black replies 10 . . . B–Q2, and if 11 Q–N4 (or R3), N–B7†.

Danish Gambit

	WHITE	BLACK
1	P-K4	P-K4
2	P-Q4	PxP
3	P-QB3	PxP
4	B-QB4	PxP
5	BxP	P-Q4
6	BxQP	N-KB3
7	N-QB3[1]	NxB
8	NxN	P-QB3?[2]
	see diagram	
9	N-B6†[3]	. . . .

White wins decisive material

WHITE TO PLAY

With a Pawn to the good, Black intends to swap Queens. He does. However, things do not work out as intended.

---

[1] The usual move, leading to approximate equality, is 7 BxP†, KxB; 8 QxQ, B-N5†; 9 Q-Q2, BxQ†.

[2] A blunder. First 8 . . . N-Q2 and then 9 . . . P-QB3 would allow Black to retain his extra Pawn with safety.

[3] And White wins. If 9 . . . PxN; 10 QxQ†, KxQ; 11 BxP† and 12 BxR or 9 . . . K-K2; 10 B-R3†, K-K3; 11 QxQ, B-N5†; 12 BxB, RxQ; 13 N-R5 or 13 N-N4 and White has won a full piece. Or even stronger in this line after 10 . . . K-K3; 11 Q-N4†, KxN; 12 P-K5†, and Black is soon mated.

Dutch Defense

	WHITE	BLACK
1	P-Q4	P-KB4
2	P-K4	PxP
3	N-QB3	N-KB3
4	P-B3	P-Q4
5	PxP	PxP
6	B-QB4	B-B4
7	KN-K2	Q-Q2
8	O-O	N-B3
9	B-KN5	O-O-O?[1]
10	P-Q5	N-K4[2]
11	Q-Q4![3]	....

see diagram

11	....	NxB
12	QxRP!	N-N3
13	P-QR4![4]	Resigns

White has an overwhelming attack

BLACK TO PLAY

With a double attack on Black's Knight and Rook Pawn, Black's choice is limited. And Black is in for a surprise.

---

[1] 9 ... P-K3 is correct.

[2] 10 ... N-QN1 is a little better, but Black can hardly cope with the White attack.

[3] Very pretty. Black must capture the Bishop, for 11 ... N-B3 is met by 12 Q-B5!

[4] By virtue of the threat of 14 P-R5 and mate at R8, White will regain his piece and remain with an overwhelming attack. Note that Black's Queen at Q2 is burdened by having to defend the Bishop at KB4, e.g. 13 ... KNxP; 14 P-R5, NxN; 15 NxN and Black is helpless.

22

	WHITE	BLACK
1	P-Q4	P-KB4
2	P-QB4	N-KB3
3	N-QB3	P-KN3
4	P-B3	P-Q4
5	PxP	NxP
6	P-K4	NxN
7	PxN	B-N2
8	B-QB4	P-B4
9	N-K2	N-B3
10	B-K3	PxQP
11	BPxP	PxP
12	PxP	R-B1
13	Q-N3[1]	BxP?[2]

see diagram

WHITE TO PLAY

Thinking he has won a Pawn as a result of his fine play, Black takes the bait. He will soon be disillusioned.

14	BxB	NxB
15	NxN	QxN
16	Q-R4†[3]	. . . .

Black will lose his Queen

[1] Both sides have treated the opening very originally. White perhaps enjoys a minimal advantage because of his central Pawn duo. Now White baits a clever trap.

[2] Black bites. He should play 13 . . . N-QR4; 14 Q-R4†, B-Q2; 15 B-N5, N-B3! With an interesting game in prospect.

[3] White wins the Queen, for if 16 . . . K-Q1; 17 R-Q1, while 16 . . . B-Q2; 17 B-B7† does the job.

Falkbeer Counter Gambit 23

	WHITE	BLACK
1	P-K4	P-K4
2	P-KB4	P-Q4
3	KPxP	P-K5
4	P-Q3	N-KB3
5	PxP	NxKP
6	N-KB3	B-QB4
7	Q-K2	P-B4[1]
8	KN-Q2[2]	O-O
9	NxN	PxN
10	B-K3	QxP[3]
	see diagram	
11	Q-B4[4]	. . . .

White wins decisive material

WHITE TO PLAY

Black seems to have solved all his opening problems; he has recovered his Gambit Pawn, and his development looks fine. All, however, is not what it seems.

---

[1] 7 . . . B-B4 is best, and Black has excellent compensation for the sacrificed Pawn.

[2] Here a simple way for White to obtain the better position is 8 B-K3, e.g. 8 . . . QxP; 9 BxB, QxB; 10 N-B3.

[3] A blunder. After 10 . . . B-KN5; 11 QxB, BxB, Black is still in the game.

[4] White wins a Bishop, for after 11 . . . QxQ, White recaptures 12 BxQ with check, and then 13 BxB.

24 *Falkbeer Counter Gambit*

	WHITE	BLACK
1	P-K4	P-K4
2	P-KB4	P-Q4
3	KPxP	PxP
4	N-KB3	N-KB3
5	P-Q4[1]	NxP
6	P-B4	B-N5†
7	QN-Q2	N-K6
8	Q-R4†[2]	B-Q2
9	Q-N3[3]	Q-K2
10	K-B2	N-Q8†
11	K-N1[4]	. . . .

see diagram

| 11 | . . . . | N-B6 |
| 12 | P-KR3[5] | B-R5 |

White's Queen is lost

BLACK TO PLAY

After tall maneuvering, Black has a strong initiative. But he has easy victory in his grasp. Do you see it?

---

[1] Either 5 P–QB4 or 5 N–B3 should be played. Now it will not be easy for White to recover his Gambit Pawn.

[2] 8 Q–N3 is a slight improvement.

[3] Of course 9 QxB loses to 9 . . . N–B7†.

[4] If 11 QxN, Q–K6 mate.

[5] The threat was 12 . . . Q–K6 mate, and if 12 N–N1, B–R5 traps the Queen as in the game.

Four Knight's Game

	WHITE	BLACK
1	P-K4	P-K4
2	N-KB3	N-QB3
3	N-B3	N-B3
4	B-B4	B-B4[1]
5	P-Q3	P-Q3
6	O-O	O-O[2]
7	B-KN5	B-KN5[3]
8	N-Q5	N-Q5
9	Q-Q2	Q-Q2[4]
10	BxN	BxN

see diagram

11	N-K7†	K-R1
12	BxP†	KxB
13	Q-N5†	K-R1
14	Q-B6[5]	. . . .

**Black has been
checkmated**

WHITE TO PLAY

*Imitation may be flattery, but
here it is the path to being
checkmated.*

---

[1] 4 . . . NxP and if 5 NxN, P-Q4 is a good line for Black.

[2] 6 . . . B-KN5 is more promising for Black.

[3] The policy of imitation is extremely hazardous as the sequel demonstrates.

[4] Black has better chances of defending with 9 . . . P-QB3 and if 10 NxN†, PxN; 11 B-R4, BxN; 12 Q-R6, N-K7†; 13 K-R1, BxP†; 14 KxB, N-B5†; 15 K-R1, N-N3.

[5] And Black is mated.

Four Knight's Game

	WHITE	BLACK
1	P-K4	N-KB3
2	N-QB3	P-K4
3	N-B3	N-B3
4	B-N5	B-N5
5	O-O	O-O
6	P-Q3	P-Q3
7	N-K2	B-N5
8	P-B3	B-QB4
9	N-N3	B-N3
10	P-KR3	B-Q2
11	B-N5	N-K2¹
12	BxN	BxB²
	see diagram	
13	N-R5!	PxB
14	Q-Q2	K-R1
15	Q-R6	N-B4³
16	PxN	R-KN1
17	NxP	R-N2
18	N-N5	. . . .⁴

WHITE TO PLAY

Black appears to have put up a reasonably good defense. It is not good enough, for White has a crushing combination.

White wins decisive material

---

¹ A serious mistake which costs the game. Black could defend with 11 . . . P-KR3; 12 B-KR4, K-R2 (not 12 . . . P-KN4; 13 NxNP!) and 13 . . . R-KN1.

² 12 . . . PxB; 13 N-R5, K-R1 is somewhat better, for if 14 Q-Q2, N-KN1 holds; so White must play 14 BxB, QxB; 15 NxBP, Q-K3; 16 NxRP, R-KN1 or 16 N-N4 and Black has counter-chances for his material deficit.

³ Naturally if 15 . . . R-KN1; 16 QxBP† and 17 QxR mate.

⁴ There is no defense to 19 N(5)xRP followed by 20 N-N5, mating or winning the Queen.

French Defense

	WHITE	BLACK
1	P-Q4	P-Q4
2	N-QB3	N-KB3
3	B-N5	P-K3[1]
4	P-K4	B-K2
5	BxN	BxB
6	P-K5	B-K2
7	Q-N4	O-O
8	B-Q3	N-B3
9	N-B3	N-N5
10	O-O-O	NxB†
11	RxN	P-QB4
12	PxP	BxP[2]
13	N-K4	B-K2
14	N/3-N5	P-KR3
15	P-KR4	Q-B2?[3]

see diagram

WHITE TO PLAY

Black has played the opening to gain the minute advantage of the Bishop-pair. But he has neglected his King, and now White comes crashing through.

16	N-B6†	BxN[4]
17	PxB	P-KN3[5]
18	P-R5	Q-K4[6]
19	N-R7!	KxN[7]
20	PxP†[8]	. . . .

White has a winning attack

[1] 3 . . . B–B4 here gives Black an easier game than he generally obtains in the French.

[2] 12 . . . P–QN3 to recapture with the Pawn is a worthwhile idea. Then if 13 PxP, QxP and Black has some Queen-side files on which to work for attack, and he is threatening the White KBP.

[3] White has built up a strong attack and Black should try 15 . . . P–B4; if 16 PxP e.p., BxP; 17 NxP?, Q–K2 and Black would appear to have adequate defensive resources.

[4] Certainly not 16 . . . PxN; 17 NxP† and 18 Q–N7 mate. However, 16 . . . K–R1 may be a little better than 16 . . . BxN.

[5] If 17 . . . PxN; 18 QxP, P–KN3; 19 Q–R6.

[6] Again 18 . . . PxN; 19 QxP wins easily.

[7] If the Rook moves, 20 PxP is decisive.

[8] White wins. If 20 . . . K–N1; 21 PxP†, KxP; 22 Q–N7†, K–K1; 23 Q–K7 mate. If 20 . . . K–R1; 21 RxP†, K–N1; 22 PxP†, KxP; 23 Q–N6 mate, and if 20 . . . PxP; 21 RxP†, KxR (or 21 . . . K–N1 22 QxP mate); 22 R–R3†, Q–R4; 23 RxQ†, PxR; 24 Q–N7 mate.

French Defense

	WHITE	BLACK
1	P-K4	P-K3
2	P-Q4	P-Q4
3	N-QB3	N-KB3
4	P-K5	KN-Q2
5	Q-N4[1]	P-QB4
6	B-KN5?[2]	Q-N3
7	O-O-O	PxP
8	RxP	NxP?[3]
	see diagram	
9	NxP!	Q-R4[4]
10	Q-Q1	QN-B3[5]
11	B-N5	PxN[6]
12	RxP	Q-B2[7]
13	R-Q8†	....

White mates on the next move

WHITE TO PLAY

Black thought he earned the King Pawn as a reward for his sound play. The impetuous capture, however, will convert reward to punishment.

[1] The Gledhill Attack, which frequently features the speculative sacrifice of a Pawn.
[2] 6 N-B3 or 6 B-K3 offers somewhat better chances than this dubious sacrifice.
[3] Black is too impatient. First 8 ... QN-B3! would enable him to win the KP.
[4] Now 8 ... NxQ; 9 NxQ and White is threatening 10 R-Q8 mate.
[5] Not 10 ... QxP?; 11 N-B7 mate or 10 ... PxN; 11 RxP and White threatens mate at Q8 as well as the Queen.
[6] If 11 ... B-Q2; 12 R-R4 and the Queen is trapped (12 ... QxB 13 N-B7†).
[7] White threatened 13 BxN† winning the Queen, as well as his actual 13th move (R-Q8†).

French Defense

	WHITE	BLACK
1	P-K4	P-K3
2	P-Q4	P-Q4
3	N-QB3	B-N5
4	P-K5	P-QB4
5	P-QR3	BxN†
6	PxB	Q-B2
7	N-B3	N-K2
8	B-Q3	QN-B3
9	O-O	O-O?[1]
	see diagram	
10	BxP†![2]	....

White has a winning attack

WHITE TO PLAY

This stock sacrifice in this and similar positions numbers many neophytes among its victims.

---

[1] 9 ... B-Q2 or 9 ... P-B5 yield approximate equality. The text allows a winning sacrifice.

[2] This wins, e.g. 10 ... KxB; 11 N-N5†, K-N1; 12 Q-R5, R-Q1; 13 QxP†, K-R1; 14 P-KB4!, Q-Q2; 15 R-B3, N-B4; 16 R-R3†, N-R3; 17 Q-N6, K-N1; 18 RxN followed by 19 R-R8† and 20 Q-R7 mate, or 11 ... K-N3; 12 Q-N4, P-B3 (if 12 ... P-B4; 13 Q-R4, P-B5; 14 Q-R7†, KxN; 15 P-R4†, K-N5; 16 P-B3†, K-N6; 17 B-Q2 followed by 18 B-K1 mate); 13 NxP†, K-B2; 14 QxP†, KxN; 15 QxR, etc. A very attractive version of a familiar sacrifice.

30 *French Defense*

	WHITE	BLACK
1	P-K4	P-K3
2	P-Q4	P-Q4
3	N-QB3	B-N5
4	B-Q2	PxP
5	Q-N4	QxP
6	O-O-O	P-KB4
7	B-KN5!¹	Q-K4
8	R-Q8†	K-B2
9	N-B3!	Q-R4?²
	see diagram	
10	B-N5!!³	N-KB3⁴
11	Q-R5†!!⁵	. . . .

WHITE TO PLAY

A classic example of the double-edged nature of Pawn-grabbing. White's gain in time converts to a powerful gain in development.

Black cannot avoid checkmate

---

¹ White plays the whole game in a va banque manner and succeeds beautifully. Now if 7 . . . PxQ; 8 RxQ and White will recapture the gambited Pawns.

² The losing move, which allows a beautiful refutation. Correct was 9 . . . PxN; 10 QxB, Q-K8†!; 11 R-Q1, N-QB3; 12 Q-KR4 with fair attacking possibilities.

³ Very elegant. White cuts off the Queen from the defense of the K4 square and threatens 11 N-K5 mate.

⁴ 10 . . . N-QB3 loses to 11 N-K5†, NxN; 12 B-K8†, K-B1; 13 B-N6 or R5 mate.

⁵ A problem-like conclusion which forces checkmate. Now if 11 . . . NxQ; 12 N-K5 mates. If 11 . . . K-K2; 12 R-K8†, K-Q3 (or 12 . . . RxR; 13 QxR† 13 . . . K-Q3; 14 Q-B8 mate); 13 R-Q1†, N-Q4 (if 13 . . . K-B4; 14 B-K3 mates); 14 B-K7 mate. If 11 . . . P-N3; 12 N-K5†, K-K2 (if 12 . . . K-N2 White mates at KR6); 13 QxP†!, RxQ (13 . . . KxR; 14 BxN† and 15 QxB or 15 QxR mates); 14 R-K8†, K-Q3; 15 N-B4†, K-B4; 16 B-K3 mate.

	WHITE	BLACK
1	P-K4	P-K3
2	P-Q4	P-Q4
3	N-QB3	B-N5
4	Q-N4[1]	N-KB3
5	QxP	R-N1
6	Q-R6	NxP
7	QxP?[2]	R-B1
8	B-Q2[3]	. . . .

see diagram

8	. . . .	BxN
9	BxB	Q-B3[4]

Black wins decisive material

BLACK TO PLAY
White's Pawn-grabbing expedition here goes awry.

---

[1] 4 P-K5 followed by 5 P-QR3 is the line of play recommended by the theoreticians. The text is not good as it loses time and results in the exchange of a valuable central Pawn for a less important wing Pawn.

[2] This is a serious error. 7 KN-K2 or 7 P-QR3 are preferable alternatives.

[3] If 8 Q-R3, P-K4! is very strong.

[4] Black will win Queen for Rook. The threat is 10 . . . QxP†; 11 K-Q1, QxB† as well as 10 . . . R-R1 winning the Queen.

	WHITE	BLACK
1	P-K4	P-K3
2	P-Q4	P-Q4
3	N-QB3	B-N5
4	N-K2	PxP
5	P-QR3	BxN†
6	NxB	P-KB4[1]
7	P-B3	PxP
8	QxP	QxP
9	Q-N3	N-KB3[2]
10	QxNP	Q-K4†
11	B-K2	R-N1
12	Q-R6	R-N3
13	Q-R4	B-Q2
14	B-N5	B-B3[3]
15	O-O-O	BxP[4]
	see diagram	
16	KR-K1	B-K5
17	B-R5	NxB
18	R-Q8†	K-B2
19	QxN[5]	. . . .

WHITE TO PLAY

Another sermon on the evils of Pawn-grabbing and neglected development is recorded here.

White has a winning attack

---

[1] Not recommended.

[2] 9 ... N-K2 gives much better fighting chances for successful defense.

[3] Here 14 ... N-B3 with a view towards 15 ... O-O-O was absolutely essential.

[4] Or 15 ... QN-Q2; 16 KR-K1, threatening 17 B-R5.

[5] Black's game is without resource. White threatens the sequence 20 NxB, 21 QxP†, and 22 R-B1†; Black is powerless to prevent this.

French Defense

	WHITE	BLACK
1	P-K4	P-K3
2	P-Q4	P-Q4
3	N-QB3	B-N5
4	N-K2	PxP
5	P-QR3	BxN†[1]
6	NxB	P-KB4[2]
7	P-B3	PxP
8	QxP	Q-R5†
9	P-N3	QxQP
10	B-K3	Q-B3
11	O-O-O	N-B3
12	B-QN5	B-Q2
13	P-KR4	P-QR3[3]
	see diagram	
14	RxB	KxR
15	B-N5	Q-K4
16	R-Q1†	K-B1[4]
17	BxN	PxB
18	QxQBP[5]	. . . .

WHITE TO PLAY

As is usual in traps, the issue is material versus development. Superior development must act before material consolidates.

Black cannot avoid mate

[1] Or 5 ... B-K2; 6 NxP, N-QB3; 7 B-K3, N-B3; 8 KN-B3, O-O with equal chances.

[2] This policy of keeping the extra Pawn at all costs is not recommended. Black can equalize here by 6 ... N-QB3; 7 B-QN5, N-K2; 8 O-O, O-O.

[3] Black should continue with his development by 13 ... KN-K2, and though White has compensation for the sacrificed Pawns, Black is by no means lost.

[4] 16 ... K-K1; 17 BxN†, PxB; 18 QxP† and 19 QxR is likewise hopeless for Black.

[5] White threatens not only 19 QxR†, but also 19 R-Q8 mate. Black is lost.

34 *French Defense*

	WHITE	BLACK
1	P-K4	P-K3
2	P-Q4	P-Q4
3	N-QB3	B-N5
4	B-Q3	N-KB3
5	B-KN5	PxP
6	BxP	P-B4
7	N-B3	PxP[1]
8	NxP	Q-R4
9	BxN	BxN†
10	PxB	QxP†
11	Q-Q2!	QxR†?[2]
12	K-K2	QxR
	see diagram	
13	NxP!![3]	....

White has a winning attack

WHITE TO PLAY

Black has swallowed more than he can digest. Now, with one fell move, it is over.

---

[1] Immediately 8 . . . Q–R4 is better for Black.

[2] 11 . . . QxQ†; 12 KxQ, PxB; 13 QR–N1! and if 13 . . . P–K4; 14 RxP! is good for White, but at least Black has some drawing chances. Accepting the double Rook sacrifice leaves him without resource.

[3] There is no defense, e.g. 13 . . . PxN; 14 Q–Q8†, K–B2; 15 Q–K7†, K–N1; 16 QxP or Q–K8 mate, or 13 . . . PxB; 14 Q–Q8 mate, or 13 . . . N–B3; 14 BxN†, PxB 15; Q–Q8 mate. And 13 . . . B–Q2; 14 NxP†, K–B1; 15 Q–Q6†, K–N1; 16 N–K6!, PxN (forced; White threatened both 17 Q–B8 mate and 17 Q–N3 mate); 17 Q–N3†, K–B2 or B1; 18 Q–N7†, K–K1; 19 Q–K7 mate. Finally, if 13 . . . N–Q2; 14 NxP†, K–B1; 15 Q–Q6†, K–N1; 16 N–B5 (threatening 17 N–R6 mate), P–KR4 (if 16 . . . NxB; 17 Q–Q8 mate); 17 Q–N3†, K–B1; 18 Q–N7†, K–K1; 19 N–Q6 mate.

French Defense

	WHITE	BLACK
1	P-K4	P-K3
2	P-Q4	P-Q4
3	N-Q2	P-QB4
4	P-QB3[1]	BPxP
5	BPxP	PxP
6	NxP	B-Q2[2]
7	N-KB3	B-B3
8	B-Q3	N-B3
9	NxN†	QxN[3]
	see diagram	
10	B-KN5	BxN
11	Q-B1[4]	....

White wins decisive material

WHITE TO PLAY

On the surface, White cannot win the Queen on account of the reply . . . BxN. What is the flaw in this reasoning?

---

[1] 4 PxQP or 4 KN–B3 is considered better for White.

[2] Weak. 6 . . . KN–B3 gives Black a good game, for after the exchange of Knights, Black will gain further time by the threat of . . . B–N5†, and then he can concentrate on the isolated White QP.

[3] 9 . . . PxN was necessary. The Queen is now lost.

[4] If 11 . . . QxP; 12 Q–B8† with mate next.

36

French Defense

	WHITE	BLACK
1	P-K4	P-K3
2	P-Q4	P-Q4
3	N-Q2	P-QB4
4	KPxP	KPxP
5	PxP[1]	BxP
6	N-K2?[2]	....
	see diagram	
6	....	Q-N3[3]

Black wins overwhelming material

BLACK TO PLAY

White's last offbeat move to confuse his opponent boomerangs.

---

[1] 5 B–N5† or 5 KN–B3 gives White a good game.

[2] 6 B–Q3 still yields approximate equality.

[3] Black wins at least a piece, for if the King Knight moves to any square but Q4, 7 . . . BxP† is followed by 8 . . . Q–K6 mate, and if the Queen Knight moves anywhere except K4 or QB4, the same 7 . . . BxP† and 8 . . . Q–K6 mate occur.

French Defense

	WHITE	BLACK
1	P-K4	P-K3
2	P-Q4	P-Q4
3	N-QB3	PxP
4	NxP	N-Q2
5	N-KB3	KN-B3
6	NxN†	NxN
7	B-Q3	B-K2
8	Q-K2	O-O
9	B-KN5	P-QN3?[1]

see diagram

10	BxN	BxB
11	Q-K4[2]	....

White wins decisive material

WHITE TO PLAY

Here is a standard winning opening combination which occurs frequently.

---

[1] A careless move which loses quickly. 9 . . . P–B4, and if 10 PxP, Q–R4† and 11 . . . QxBP is a reasonable line of play.

[2] Black must defend against 12 QxP mate, so White will win the Queen Rook.

	WHITE	BLACK
1	P-K4	P-K3
2	P-Q4	P-Q4
3	N-QB3	PxP
4	NxP	N-Q2
5	N-KB3	KN-B3
6	KN-N5[1]	B-K2
7	NxBP	KxN
8	N-N5†	K-N1
9	NxKP	Q-K1
10	NxBP?[2]	....
	see diagram	
10	....	B-N5†[3]

BLACK TO PLAY

Up to the diagrammed position, Black has been on the receiving end. Now Black gives once — and it is over.

White has been checkmated

---

[1] Careless play; either 6 ... NxN or 6 ... P-KR3 is satisfactory for Black.

[2] With 10 B-QB4 White has a winning position; the threatened discovered check is devastating and if 10 ... B-N5†; 11 K-B1! and the situation is no better for Black.

[3] Never have the tables been turned more rapidly. Now it is White who is mated.

French Defense

	WHITE	BLACK
1	P-K4	P-K3
2	P-Q4	P-Q4
3	P-K5	P-QB4
4	P-QB3	N-QB3
5	N-B3	Q-N3
6	B-Q3[1]	PxP
7	PxP	B-Q2[2]
8	O-O!?[3]	NxQP
9	NxN	QxN
10	N-B3	QxP
11	R-K1	Q-Q3
12	N-N5	BxN
13	BxB†	K-Q1
14	B-K3	N-K2
15	R-QB1	N-B4
16	B-B5	Q-B5?[4]
17	P-KN3	Q-N4
	see diagram	
18	QxP†	PxQ
19	B-N6†	....[5]

WHITE TO PLAY

Black has accepted two Gambit Pawns and forfeited castling.   Now his King is an easy target.

White mates on the next move

---

[1] With this move, White virtually commits himself to sacrificing a Pawn.

[2] But not immediately 7 . . . NxQP; 8 NxN, QxN; 9 B–N5† winning the Queen.

[3] After 8 B–K2 (if 8 B–B2, N–N5; 9 B–N3?, B–N4!); 8 . . . KN–K2 and 9 . . . N–B4 Black has a wonderful game, so White embarks on a speculative sacrifice.

[4] Black should reconcile himself to sacrificing the Queen. After 16 . . . QxB; 17 RxQ, BxR he would have a good game with Rook, Knight and two Pawns and a safe position for the Queen.

[5] And White will mate with 20 R–K8†.

40

	WHITE	BLACK
1	P-KB4	P-K4
2	PxP	P-Q3
3	PxP	BxP
4	N-KB3	P-KN4
5	P-Q4	P-N5
6	N-N5	P-KB4
7	P-K4	B-K2¹
	see diagram	
8	N-KR3	PxN?
9	Q-R5†	K-B1
10	B-QB4	Q-K1²
11	Q-R6†	NxQ
12	BxB	....

WHITE TO PLAY

White has entrapped his own Knight as he picked off a Pawn. Is there a way out for him in this dilemma?

Black has been checkmated

---

¹ 7 . . . P-KR3 is better, with a very difficult game in prospect for both sides.

² The only chance to continue play is by 10 . . . B-N5†; 11 P-B3, Q-K2; 12 P-K5!, B-K3; 13 BxB, QxB; 14 PxB, N-QB3; 15 O-O! and White should win, but there are still possibilities to err.

Giuoco Piano

	WHITE	BLACK
1	P-K4	P-K4
2	N-KB3	N-QB3
3	B-B4	B-B4
4	P-B3	N-B3
5	P-Q4	PxP
6	PxP	B-N5†
7	N-B3	NxKP
8	O-O	NxN
9	PxN	BxP
	see diagram	
10	Q-N3![1]	BxR?[2]
11	BxP†	K-B1[3]
12	B-N5	N-K2
13	N-K5	BxP
14	B-N6	P-Q4[4]
15	Q-B3†	B-B4
16	BxB	BxN
17	B-K6†	B-B3
18	BxB	Q-N1[5]
19	B-N5†	K-K1
20	Q-B7†	K-Q1
21	BxN	....

**Black has been
checkmated**

WHITE TO PLAY

*Black has won two Pawns (at
the cost of development) and
threatens a Rook. If White
delays his initiative by con-
serving material, Black gets
the better of it. But White
has a crushing rejoinder.*

---

[1] 10 B-R3, and if 10 . . . P-Q4, (not 10 BxR?; 11 R-K1†) ; 11 B-N5 is
also very promising for White, since Black will have trouble with his
King in the center of the board.

[2] Black can equalize here by returning his extra Pawns as follows:
10 . . . P-Q4; 11 BxP, O-O; 12 BxP†, K-R1; 13 QxB, RxB; 14 N-K5,
NxN; 15 PxN, B-K3. The text loses.

[3] Or 11 . . . K-K2; 12 B-N5† winning the Queen.

[4] 15 Q-B7 mate had to be prevented.

[5] Or 18 . . . PxB; 19 QxP†, K-K1; 20 Q-B7 mate.

	WHITE	BLACK
1	P-K4	P-K4
2	N-KB3	N-QB3
3	B-B4	B-B4
4	P-B3	N-B3
5	P-Q4	PxP
6	PxP	B-N5†
7	N-B3	NxKP
8	O-O	BxN
9	P-Q5	N-K4[1]
10	PxB	NxB
11	Q-Q4	N/B-Q3[2]
	see diagram	
12	QxNP	Q-B3
13	QxQ	NxQ
14	R-K1†	K-Q1[3]
15	B-N5	N-K1
16	RxN†	KxR[4]
17	R-K1†	K-B1
18	B-R6†	K-N1
19	R-K5[5]	. . . .

White mates shortly

WHITE TO PLAY

Black has played 11 . . . N/B–Q3, seemingly retaining his extra piece; but White has a surprise continuation which leads to a forced win.

---

[1] Another recommended line for Black here is 9 . . . B–B3; 10 R–K1, N–K2; 11 RxN, P–Q3; 12 B–N5, BxB; 13 NxB, O–O.
[2] This loses. The right move is 11 . . . P–KB4; 12 QxN, P–Q3; 13 N–Q4, O–O when Black has an extra Pawn to compensate him for the White initiative.
[3] For 14 . . . K–B1 refer to trap 43.
[4] Or 16 . . . RxR; 17 BxN†, R–K2; 18 R–K1 winning.
[5] There is no defense to mate. The threat is 20 R–N5 mate, and if the Black Knight moves, 20 R–K8 is mate.

Giuoco Piano

WHITE	BLACK
1 P-K4	P-K4
2 N-KB3	N-QB3
3 B-B4	B-B4
4 P-B3	N-B3
5 P-Q4	PxP
6 PxP	B-N5†
7 N-B3	NxKP
8 O-O	BxN
9 P-Q5	N-K4
10 PxB	NxB
11 Q-Q4	N/B5-Q3?[1]
12 QxNP	Q-B3
see diagram	
13 QxQ	NxQ
14 R-K1†	K-B1
15 B-R6†	K-N1
16 R-K5	N/B3-K5[2]
17 R-K1	P-KB4[3]
18 R-K7	P-N3
19 N-R4![4]	....

White has a winning attack

WHITE TO PLAY

Though Black's King is badly confined, his Knights appear to be staunch defenders until reinforcements can arrive. White demolishes Black's hopes by simple developing moves.

[1] For other comments about the opening, see the preceding game.

[2] Or 16 . . . N(Q3)-K5; 17 N-Q2, P-Q3; 18 NxN and wins, e.g. 18 . . . NxN; 19 R-K8 mate or 18 . . . PxR; 19 NxN mate.

[3] Necessary since White threatened 18 QRxN, NxR; 19 R-K8 mate.

[4] Black is lost, e.g. 19 . . . B-N2; 20 P-B3, N-B2; 21 NxP, N(K5)-Q3; 22 R-K8†, RxR; 23 RxR†, NxR; 24 N-K7 mate.

44

	WHITE	BLACK
1	P-K4	P-K4
2	N-KB3	N-QB3
3	B-B4	B-B4
4	P-B3	B-N3
5	P-Q4	Q-K2
6	O-O	P-Q3
7	N-N5	N-R3
8	B-K3	O-O
9	P-B4	PxQP
10	PxP	N-KN5
11	P-B5	NxB?[1]
	see diagram	
12	Q-R5	P-KR3
13	P-B6[2]	. . . .

WHITE TO PLAY

Black's Knight has captured a Bishop and threatens three more White pieces. But Black is destined to die in a strange manner — choking on too many pins.

Black will be checkmated or lose his Queen

---

[1] Black should play 11 ... BxQP; 12 BxB (not 12 QxN, BxB†; 13 K–R1, QxN); 12 ... QxN and Black is a Pawn ahead with a defensible game.

[2] If 13 ... PxP; 14 Q–N6†, etc.

Giuoco Piano *Evans Gambit*

	WHITE	BLACK
1	P-K4	P-K4
2	N-KB3	N-QB3
3	B-B4	B-B4
4	P-QN4	BxP
5	P-B3	B-R4
6	P-Q4	PxP
7	O-O	P-Q3[1]
8	Q-N3	Q-K2[2]
9	P-K5!	PxKP
10	B-R3	Q-B3
11	PxP	P-K5
12	P-Q5!	PxN
13	PxN	BPxP
14	R-Q1	B-N3?[3]
	see diagram	
15	BxP†	QxB
16	R-Q8†	. . . .[4]

Black's Queen is lost

WHITE TO PLAY

Black threatens mate on the move or the win of a Rook. But White's reply proves that chess is based on justice. Black is fatally punished for neglecting development.

---

[1] The correct order of moves is 7 . . . B-N3; 8 PxP, P-Q3. This takes the sting out of Q-N3 for White by allowing Black to reply with . . . N-QR4.

[2] Or 8 . . . Q-B3; 9 P-K5, Q-N3; 10 R-K1, KN-K2; 11 B-R3 with a strong White attack.

[3] If 14 . . . N-K2; 15 BxP† wins as in the text, and 14 . . . N-R3; 15 PxP, BxP, and 17 B-N5† will be deadly. If 14 . . . B-K3; 15 PxP, R-Q1; 16 B-N5†, B-Q2; 17 BxB†, RxB; 18 P-N8=Q†.

[4] White wins a Queen in an overwhelming position.

	WHITE	BLACK
1	P-K4	P-K4
2	N-KB3	N-QB3
3	B-B4	B-B4
4	O-O	N-B3
5	P-Q3	P-Q3
6	B-KN5	B-KN5
7	P-KR3	P-KR4
8	PxB?[1]	PxP
9	N-R2?[2]	P-N6
10	N-KB3	....
	see diagram	
10	....	N-KN5![3]
11	BxQ	BxP†
12	RxB	PxR†
13	K-B1	R-R8†
14	K-K2	RxQ
15	KN-Q2[4]	N-Q5†
16	KxR	N-K6†
17	K-B1	N-K7 mate

**White has been
checkmated**

BLACK TO PLAY

*White hopes to weather the
storm by giving up the Exchange, remaining with superior material. Black shows
how the right Knight at the
right square at the right time
is worth more than a Queen.*

---

[1] This capture, which opens the Rook file, is too dangerous.
[2] Better possibilities of defense are offered by 9 KN–Q2 or 9 N–R4.
[3] The Queen offer justifies the preceding sacrifice.
[4] Naturally White must try to prevent 15 . . . P–B8=Q†, but the text
leads to a beautiful semi-smothered mate.

Giuoco Piano *Max Lange Attack*

	WHITE	BLACK
1	P-K4	P-K4
2	N-KB3	N-QB3
3	B-B4	B-B4
4	O-O	N-B3
5	P-Q4	PxP[1]
6	P-K5	P-Q4
7	PxN	PxB
8	R-K1†	B-K3
9	N-N5	Q-Q4[2]
10	N-QB3	Q-B4[3]
11	N/3-K4	B-KB1?[4]

see diagram

12	NxBP	KxN[5]
13	N-N5†	K-N1[6]
14	P-KN4!	QxP/3[7]
15	RxB	Q-Q1
16	Q-B3	Q-Q2
17	R-K7!	....[8]

Black cannot avoid checkmate

WHITE TO PLAY

It seems that Black has over-come the worst with a Pawn plus, but the power of White's Pawn on the sixth rank over-whelms him.

---

[1] In this opening sequence 5 . . . BxP is good for Black, as White doesn't get enough play for the sacrificed Pawn.

[2] Not 9 . . . QxP; 10 NxB, PxN; 11 Q-R5† followed by 12 QxB winning a piece.

[3] And certainly not 10 . . . PxN as after 11 QxQ, Black's Bishop is pinned and he can't recapture.

[4] Black should play 11 . . . O-O-O with chances for both sides. The text is a mistake but he wants to guard against 12 PxP, KR-N1; 13 P-KN4, Q-K4 (or 13 . . . QxNP†; 14 QxQ, BxQ; 15 N-B6 wins); 14 P-B4, Q-Q4; 15 N-B6† and wins the Queen.

[5] If 12 . . . BxN; 13 N-Q6† wins the Queen.

[6] Or 13 . . . KxP; 14 RxB† wins.

[7] Or 14 . . . QxNP†; 15 QxQ, BxQ; 16 P-B7 mate, or 14 . . . Q-Q4; 15 RxB winning.

48 *Gruenfeld Defense*

	WHITE	BLACK
1	P-Q4	N-KB3
2	P-QB4	P-KN3
3	N-QB3	P-Q4
4	Q-N3	PxP
5	QxBP	B-K3
6	Q-N5†[1]	N-B3
7	N-B3	N-Q4
8	QxP?[2]	N/4-N5
9	B-B4	B-R3!
10	BxP[3]	....
	see diagram	
10	....	NxQP
11	BxQ[4]	N/Q5-B7†
12	K-Q1	RxB†
13	N-Q5	BxN
14	Q-B7	BxN†
15	QxR†	KxQ
16	KPxB	K-B2[5]

White has a winning attack

BLACK TO PLAY

Does the old adage prove false here: "He who grabs the Queen Knight's Pawn sleeps in the streets"? Apparently, White's greed has been rewarded by the capture of another Pawn. But the Pawn-snatcher has a grim surprise awaiting him.

---

[1] Better is 6 Q–Q3 followed by an early P–K4.
[2] This loses. White should play 8 NxN, BxN; 9 P–K3.
[3] If 10 BxB, QR–N1 traps the Queen.
[4] 11 NxN, QxN and Black threatens mates at both QB7 and Q7.
[5] Black wins at least another piece, for 17 QR–N1 is met by 17 . . . R–Q1† and now 18 K–K2, R–Q7 mate.

Gruenfeld Defense

	WHITE	BLACK
1	P-Q4	N-KB3
2	P-QB4	P-KN3
3	N-QB3	P-Q4
4	N-B3	B-N2
5	Q-N3	PxP
6	QxBP	O-O
7	P-K4	N-R3
8	P-K5	B-K3?[1]

see diagram

9	PxN![2]	BxQ
10	PxB	KxP
11	BxB[3]	. . . .

**White has superiority in
material and position**

WHITE TO PLAY

*Intent on gaining a sharp
tempo, Black forgets that a
Pawn captures diagonally forward and devours everything
in its slanting path.*

---

[1] This is a mistake which spoils the Black position, which is actually
quite promising after 8 . . . KN–Q2; 9 Q–N3, N–N3; 10 BxN, PxB;
11 B–K3, B–K3; 12 Q–B2, N–Q4; 13 O–O, NxB; 14 PxN, P–QB4; 15
P–Q5, B–N5; 16 Q–K4, BxN; 17 PxB, R–N1 and Black threatens
both RxP and R–N5.

[2] A surprise.

[3] And White has gained three pieces for Queen and Pawn in a position
highly favorable for the pieces.

	WHITE	BLACK
1	P-Q4	N-KB3
2	P-QB4	P-KN3
3	N-QB3	P-Q4
4	PxP	NxP
5	P-K4	NxN
6	PxN	P-QB4
7	B-QB4	B-N2
8	N-K2	PxP
9	PxP	N-B3
10	B-K3[1]	Q-R4†
11	B-Q2	Q-R6
12	R-QN1[2]	O-O[3]
13	P-Q5[4]	N-K4
14	B-N4?[5]	....
	see diagram	
14	....	Q-B6!![6]
15	PxQ?[7]	NxP†
16	K-B1	B-R6

**White has been
checkmated**

BLACK TO PLAY

*Black's salvation is to jump
from the frying pan into the
fire. If he stirs the fire,
White will burn down his own
house.*

[1] The position is typical of the exchange variation of the Gruenfeld;
White has a broad Pawn center, but it is under constant pressure.
[2] A resourceful method of defending the Queen Pawn, for if 12 . . .
NxP; 13 B-N4 wins the Queen.
[3] Black also baits the hook.
[4] And he has a tug on the line. 13 O-O was better.
[5] White traps the Queen.
[6] And the fish gets away.
[7] A blunder, but other moves allow Black to play either 15 . . . QxKP
or 15 . . . QxNP, with an extra Pawn and the far superior position.

Gruenfeld Defense

	WHITE	BLACK
1	P-Q4	N-KB3
2	N-KB3	P-KN3
3	P-B4	B-N2
4	N-B3	P-Q4
5	P-K3	O-O
6	B-Q3	N-B3!¹
7	P-QR3	B-N5
8	P-R3	BxN
9	QxB	P-K4!
10	BPxP	PxP
11	PxN	PxN
12	PxNP	R-N1
13	B-B4?²	N-Q2
14	P-QN3³	N-K4
15	Q-K2	....

see diagram

15	....	NxB
16	PxN⁴	P-B7
17	R-QR2⁵	B-B6†

White loses overwhelming material

BLACK TO PLAY

White has apparently dodged Black's bag of tricks. A final conjuring act on Black's part, however, illustrates the force of a passed Pawn on the seventh rank.

---

¹ An interesting innovation whereby Black aims for an eventual . . . P–K4 rather than the customary . . . P–QB4.

² Preferable is 13 Q–K2.

³ Or 14 R–QN1, P–B7; 15 R–QR1, N–K4; 16 Q–K2, NxB; 17 QxN, Q–Q8 mate.

⁴ Or 16 QxN, P–B7; 17 R–QR2, Q–Q8 mate.

⁵ If 18 B–Q2, P–B8=Q†, and if 18 K–B1, Q–Q8† and mate next.

	WHITE	BLACK
1	P-Q4	N-KB3
2	P-QB4	P-KN3
3	N-QB3	P-Q4
4	B-B4	B-N2
5	P-K3	O-O
6	R-B1	P-B4
7	PxBP	Q-R4
8	PxP	R-Q1
9	Q-Q2?[1]	....

see diagram

9	....	NxP
10	B-B7[2]	QxB
11	NxN	RxN![3]
12	QxR	B-K3
13	Q-Q2	N-B3[4]

Black has a decisive positional advantage

BLACK TO PLAY

White has been lured into a line advocated by a former world champion, where Black's loss of the Exchange is more than outweighed by his accelerated development.

---

[1] 9 B–B4! or 9 Q–R4 is preferable to the text.

[2] A brilliant mistake.

[3] This exchange sacrifice completely refutes White's opening strategy. Now White's backward development will not allow of a successful defense.

[4] Black will continue to gain time for attack with . . . R–Q1 and . . . Q–R4†. The likely continuation would be 14 R–Q1, R–Q1; 15 Q–B1, Q–R4†; 16 R–Q2, R–Q4; 17 N–K2, RxP; 18 N–B3, BxN; 19 PxB, RxP; 20 Q–N2, R–R6; 21 Q–N5, Q–B6; 22 Q–N2, Q–B4; 23 Q–N1, BxP; 24 RxB, Q–R4† as in a game between Tolush and Botvinnik, Moscow, 1939.

	WHITE	BLACK
1	P-K4	P-K4
2	N-KB3	N-QB3
3	B-B4	B-K2
4	P-Q4	PxP
5	P-B3	PxP?[1]
6	Q-Q5!	N-R3
7	BxN	O-O
8	B-QB1?[2]	....

see diagram

8	....	N-N5!
9	Q-KR5	P-Q4!
10	PxQP	N-B7†
11	K-Q1	NxR
12	NxP	P-QB3[3]

Black has a positional advantage

BLACK TO PLAY

White strives to prevent 8 ... PxP, but overlooks Black's sharp retort. If 9 Q-Q1, P-B7, etc.

[1] This mistake should lose. Black should play 5 . . . N-B3, and if 6 P-K5, N-K5 with a satisfactory game.

[2] This abject retreat gives Black fine attacking chances. White should play 8 BxP, KxB; 9 NxP with an excellent game.

[3] Black has excellent chances of rescuing his Knight at R8 and White's King is none too safe. Black has the better chances.

54   *Irregular Defense*

	WHITE	BLACK
1	P-K4	P-K4
2	N-KB3	N-QB3
3	B-B4	N-Q5
4	NxP?[1]	. . . .
	see diagram	
4	. . . .	Q-N4
5	NxBP?[2]	QxP
6	R-B1	QxKP†
7	B-K2	N-B6 mate

**White has been
checkmated**

BLACK TO PLAY

*White is hooked now. This
is a trap you can only play
once against the same opponent. Though basically naive,
it's worth a niche in every
player's repertoire.*

---

[1] 4 NxN or 4 O–O gives White the advantage.

[2] White should try 5 BxP† and 6 O–O with two Pawns and some attack
for the piece.

Irregular Defense

	WHITE	BLACK
1	P-K4	P-Q3
2	B-B4	N-Q2[1]
3	N-KB3	P-KN3
4	N-N5[2]	N-R3[3]
	see diagram	
5	BxP†	NxB
6	N-K6	. . . .

Black's Queen is trapped

WHITE TO PLAY

Black has neglected to provide for the protection of his KB2. From now on in, in order to stall off the mate, White must lose his Queen.

[1] 2 . . . N-KB3 or 2 . . . P-KN3 is preferable.
[2] 4 BxP†, as in the next example, is even stronger.
[3] This costs the Queen. White already has the better game. If 4 . . . N-K4; 5 B-N3, P-KR3; 6 P-Q4, PxN; 7 PxN and now 7 . . . PxP is met by 8 BxP† winning the game.

	WHITE	BLACK
1	P-K4	P-Q3
2	N-KB3	N-Q2
3	B-B4	P-KN3
	see diagram	
4	BxP†	KxB
5	N-N5†	K-B3[1]
6	Q-B3†	KxN
7	P-Q4†	K-R5
8	Q-R3	. . . .

Black has been checkmated

WHITE TO PLAY

Black has protected his vulnerable KB2 with the wrong Knight. But has he not followed the book advice: "Don't move the same piece twice in the opening?" Remember, every rule has its exception.

---

[1] Otherwise White wins the Queen immediately by 6 N–K6.

Irregular Defense

WHITE	BLACK
1 P-Q4	P-K4[1]
2 PxP	N-QB3
3 N-KB3	Q-K2
4 B-B4[2]	Q-N5†
5 B-Q2	QxP
6 B-B3?[3]	B-N5![4]
7 Q-Q2	. . . .

see diagram

7	BxB
8 QxB	Q-B8

White has been checkmated

BLACK TO PLAY

White will soon be punished for trying to hold on to an early Pawn capture at all costs. White has only one solace — his last move was as good as any.

---

[1] An unusual variation, the chief virtue of which is that of novelty.

[2] The simplest method of maintaining White's advantage is by 4 N–B3, NxP; 5 P–K4, when White has a fine game with 6 N–Q5 in the offing, or if 5 . . . N–B3; 6 B–KN5.

[3] This is a blunder which loses outright. White still has good chances with 6 N–B3, e.g. 6 . . . B–N5; 7 N–Q5, BxB†; 8 NxB, and besides 9 NxP†, White is ready to play 9 N–QB4 with the better game.

[4] Winning immediately. Now if 7 BxB, NxB (even stronger than 7 . . . QxR) with threats on QB7 as well as QR8.

58

	WHITE	BLACK
1	P-K4	P-K4
2	P-KB4	PxP
3	N-KB3	P-KN4
4	P-KR4	P-N5
5	N-K5	N-KB3
6	P-Q4	P-Q3
7	N-Q3	NxP
8	BxP	Q-K2
9	Q-K2	B-N2
10	P-B3	P-KR4
11	N-Q2	NxN
12	KxN	QxQ†
13	BxQ	B-B4[1]
14	KR-KB1	N-Q2[2]
15	N-N4	N-B3

see diagram

16	B-N5†	B-Q2[3]
17	QR-K1†	K-Q1
18	B-N5	BxB
19	RxN![4]	. . . .

WHITE TO PLAY

The insecure position of Black's Queen Bishop is the central cog in White's combination. A potent example of a long-range payoff based on positional maneuvering.

White wins decisive material

---

[1] Best is 13 . . . N–B3; 14 QR–K1, B–K3! and now, though White has some pressure, Black is still an important Pawn ahead.

[2] Even here 14 . . . N–B3 was better to prevent White's move of 15 N–N4.

[3] On 16 . . . P–B3; 17 NxP, PxN; 18 BxP†, K–K2; 19 BxR, RxB; 20 B–N5, White wins.

[4] White wins, e.g. if 19 . . . BxR; 20 BxB†, K–Q2; 21 R–K7†, K–Q1; 22 R–K5†, K–Q2; 23 RxB.

King's Gambit

	WHITE	BLACK
1	P-K4	P-K4
2	P-KB4	PxP
3	N-KB3	B-K2
4	B-B4	N-KB3
5	N-B3	NxP
6	N-K5	B-R5†[1]
7	P-N3	PxP
8	BxP†	K-B1
9	O-O!	PxP†
10	KxP	B-N6†
11	K-N2	NxN[2]

see diagram

| 12 | Q-R5! | Q-K2[3] |
| 13 | N-N6† | ....[4] |

White mates on his next move

WHITE TO PLAY

The culmination of White's plan is a "family" check with a Knight which wins the King, the Queen, and the King's Rook in one fell blow.

---

[1] The right way is 6 ... N-N4! followed by 7 ... P-Q3, and Black should be able to stay a safe Pawn ahead. As the play now develops, White evolves a tremendous attack.

[2] If 11 ... BxN; 12 NxN and White's attack should win.

[3] If 12 ... BxN; 13 B-Q5, B4, or N3†, K-K2; 14 QxB mate.

[4] 13 ... PxN; 14 QxR mate.

60

WHITE TO PLAY

Black's premature attack has won three Pawns, but White's counterattack nets him the game.

	WHITE	BLACK
1	P-K4	P-K4
2	P-KB4	PxP
3	N-KB3	B-K2
4	B-B4	B-R5†
5	P-N3!?[1]	PxP
6	O-O	PxP†
7	K-R1	B-K2[2]
	see diagram	
8	BxP†	KxB
9	N-K5†	K-K3[3]
10	Q-N4†	KxN
11	Q-B5†	K-Q3
12	Q-Q5	. . . .

Black has been checkmated

---

[1] 5 K–B1 gives White the better game.

[2] Here Black should play 7 . . . P–Q4! and if 8 BxP, N–KB3 or 8 PxP, B–B3, and in both cases Black has good chances of nursing his extra Pawn to eventual victory.

[3] Or 9 . . . K–K1; 10 Q–R5†, P–N3; 11 NxP, KN–B3; 12 RxN, BxR; 13 N–K5†, K–K2; 14 Q–B7†, K–Q3; 15 N–B4†, K–B4; 16 Q–Q5†, K–N5; 17 P–R3†, K–R5; 18 P–N3, or Q–R5 mate.

King's Gambit

	WHITE	BLACK
1	P-K4	P-K4
2	P-KB4	PxP
3	B-K2	P-Q4
4	PxP	N-KB3
5	P-B4	P-B3
6	P-Q4	B-N5†
7	K-B1	PxP
8	BxP	PxP!!
9	BxN?[1]	....

see diagram

9	....	N-Q4!![2]
10	B-B4[3]	Q-B3!![4]

Black maintains a positional advantage

BLACK TO PLAY

Here the obvious, but hasty move, is 9 . . . RxB. Black avoids this losing move. His deep conception regains the piece with a lasting initiative.

[1] This is a positional blunder. White anticipates only 9 . . . RxB, when 10 Q-R4† would win a piece.

[2] Black now threatens to win the Queen with 10 . . . N-K6†.

[3] 10 K-B2 is slightly better, though Black has a marked positional advantage.

[4] Black is still threatening 11 . . . N-K6† as well as 11 . . . Q or NxB. After 11 N-B3, QxB White is lost, as he is a Pawn down and his King is exposed; in addition, his Black squares are very weak.

62   King's Indian Defense

	WHITE	BLACK
1	P-Q4	N-KB3
2	P-QB4	P-KN3
3	N-QB3	B-N2
4	P-K4	P-Q3
5	P-B4	P-B4
6	P-Q5	O-O
7	N-B3	P-K3
8	B-K2	PxP
9	KPxP	R-K1
10	O-O	N-N5
11	R-K1!	B-Q5†[1]
12	NxB[2]	PxN
13	QxP	Q-R5[3]
	see diagram	
14	B-Q2!	QxP†
15	K-B1[4]	. . . .

WHITE TO PLAY

*When under fire, a player
may often solve the problem
of defense by simple development. Such is the case here.
Black has shot his bolt; the
Queen swap leaves him helpless.*

White has a winning attack

[1] White has allowed the combination because he sees the flaw in it.
Black was better advised to continue with 11 . . . B–B4, and the game
would be about equal.

[2] But not 12 K–B1?, Q–R5 winning, since 13 NxQ is met by 13 . . . NxP
mate and 13 P–KN3 is followed by 13 . . . Q–R6 mate. And after 13
QxB, NxP† wins the Queen.

[3] Black has relied on this sortie, but it is without sting. He recaptures
his Pawn only to find himself in a resignable position.

[4] Now Black finds himself in great danger on the King file, as White
threatens BxN. And after 15 . . . Q–R8†; 16 Q–N1, QxQ†; 17 KxQ
White also has 18 N–N5 as a winning threat. The Black position is
hopeless.

King's Indian Defense 63

	WHITE	BLACK
1	P-Q4	N-KB3
2	P-QB4	P-KN3
3	P-KN3	B-N2
4	B-N2	P-Q3
5	N-KB3	O-O
6	O-O	P-B4
7	N-B3	N-B3
8	PxP	PxP
9	B-K3	Q-R4
10	Q-R4?[1]	QxQ
11	NxQ	P-N3
12	N-K5?[2]	. . . .
	see diagram	
12	. . . .	NxN
13	BxR	B-Q2![3]

Black wins material

BLACK TO PLAY

White, greedy to win the exchange, overlooks the insecurity of his Queen Knight. The trap was particularly deceptive, based on the quiet and innocent-looking 11 . . . P–N3.

---

[1] Better was 10 B–Q2 when White has chances of maintaining the initiative of the first move.

[2] This blunder costs two pieces for the Rook. Black was already somewhat better off as a result of the White Knight's unfortunate position.

[3] And Black must win either the Knight or the Bishop.

	WHITE	BLACK
1	P-Q4	N-KB3
2	P-QB4	P-KN3
3	N-QB3	B-N2
4	P-K4	P-Q3
5	P-B4	O-O[1]
6	B-Q3	P-B4[2]
7	PxP	PxP
8	P-K5	B-N5?[3]
	see diagram	
9	B-K2[4]	....

White wins material

WHITE TO PLAY

With his last move, Black seems to have won a valuable tempo. White's reply shows how badly Black has calculated.

---

[1] Immediately 5 ... P–B4 and if 6 PxP, 6 ... Q–R4 gives Black a good game.

[2] A good move for Black here is 6 ... N–B3, attacking the Black squares in the White center. Then if 7 P–Q5, N–Q5 followed by 8 ... P–B4; and if 7 N–B3, B–N5, or if 7 KN–K2, P–K4!

[3] Black wants to gain a tempo before retreating his Knight, but this proves to be a mistake.

[4] Now Black must lose a piece, e.g. 9 ... QxQ†; 10 BxQ, BxB; 11 PxN or 9 ... BxB; 10 QxQ, RxQ; 11 PxN. The last line is Black's best at this point as he will get two Pawns for the piece, although he still must lose with proper play on White's part.

King's Indian Defense

	WHITE	BLACK
1	P-QB4	N-KB3
2	N-QB3	P-B4
3	N-B3	P-KN3
4	P-Q4	B-N2
5	P-K4	O-O
6	B-K2	P-Q3
7	O-O	N-R3[1]
8	P-KR3	PxP
9	NxP	B-Q2
10	B-K3	N-B4
11	Q-B2	P-QR3
12	QR-Q1	Q-N1
13	P-B4	R-B1[2]
	see diagram	
14	P-K5!	N-K1[3]
15	N-Q5[4]	. . . .

White wins decisive material

WHITE TO PLAY

Black's heavy guns, the two Rooks and the Queen are badly inactivated. Soon, the weakness of Black's Queen-side squares will lead to loss of material.

---

[1] Or 7 . . . PxP; 8 NxP, N-B3; 9 N-B2! and White has some positional advantage.

[2] Black is apparently oblivious of White's threat, and this move only adds impetus to White's advance.

[3] The point is that after 14 . . . PxP; 15 PxP Black cannot play 15 . . . QxP because of 16 B-B4, and the Black Queen is caught in the center of the board!

[4] White will win material since he threatens both 16 NxP† and 16 N-N6. If 15 . . . PxP; 16 NxP†, K-B1; 17 NxR, PxN; 18 N-N6 wins.

	WHITE	BLACK
1	P-Q4	N-KB3
2	P-QB4	P-KN3
3	N-QB3	B-N2
4	P-K4	P-Q3
5	P-B3	O-O
6	B-K3	N-QB3
7	Q-Q2	P-QR3
8	O-O-O	B-Q2
9	B-R6	Q-N1[1]
10	P-KR4	P-QN4
11	P-R5	R-Q1
12	RPxP	BPxP
13	BxB	KxB
14	Q-R6†	K-B2
	see diagram	
15	P-K5!	PxKP
16	N-K4	NxP[2]
17	N-N5†	K-K1[3]
18	QxP†[4]	....

WHITE TO PLAY

White will soon show the power of a Rook on a partly open file. But the Rook will not move until the final knock-out.

Black cannot avoid checkmate

[1] Black's Queen-side attack, apparently initiated with this move, is woefully slow compared with White's play on the opposite wing. More plausible is 9 ... P-K4, fighting for his Q5 square with a view towards exchanges.

[2] This loses immediately. A better try was 16 ... R-R1 and if 17 N-N5†, K-N1! (Not 17 ... K-K1; 18 QxP†!)

[3] If 17 ... K-N1; 18 NxP wins easily.

[4] After 18 ... PxQ; 19 R-R8†, N-N1; 20 RxN mates.

	WHITE	BLACK
1	P-K4	N-QB3
2	P-Q4	P-Q4
3	PxP[1]	QxP
4	N-KB3	B-N5
5	N-B3[2]	BxN
6	NxQ[3]	BxQ
7	NxP†	K-Q2
8	NxR	BxP
9	B-KB4[4]	. . . .

see diagram

9	. . . .	P-K4
10	PxP	B-N5†
11	K-K2[5]	KN-K2
12	P-K6†	PxP
13	N-B7	N-Q5†
14	K-K3	N/2-B4[6]

White has been checkmated

BLACK TO PLAY

White's attempt to salvage his Knight will lead to a bad end. At first sight it seems that White is better developed, but appearances are deceptive here.

---

[1] Either 3 P-K5 or 3 N-QB3, PxP; 4 P-Q5 gives White fine chances and is preferable to the text.

[2] And here White should first play 5 B-K2 (now Black cannot win a Pawn with 5 . . . BxN; 6 BxB, QxP because of 7 BxN† winning the Queen) and then later N-B3. As the play proceeds he wins the exchange, but his Knight at R8 is in great danger.

[3] Now this is necessary or White loses at least a Pawn with no compensation.

[4] An attempt to rescue his Knight, but 9 P-Q5 offers better chances.

[5] And here 11 B-Q2 was absolutely necessary, though White is probably already lost.

[6] Black's minor pieces combine to produce a lively "pure" mate.

	WHITE	BLACK
1	P-Q4	N-KB3
2	P-QB4	P-K3
3	N-QB3	B-N5
4	P-K3	P-B4
5	B-Q3	P-Q4
6	N-B3	O-O
7	O-O	QN-Q2
8	P-QR3	PxQP?[1]
	see diagram	
9	NxP/5[2]	PxN
10	PxB	PxBP
11	BxP	N-N3
12	B-N3	PxP
13	BxKP[3]	. . . .

**White has a positionally
won game**

WHITE TO PLAY

Positional traps are more subtle than combinational ones; the variations are not obvious, but elegant, based on theoretical niceties. Here, White's eventual two-Bishop edge will dominate the end-game.

[1] Either 8 . . . BxN or 8 . . . B–R4 would be preferable.
[2] This pretty move assures White of the two Bishops plus a positional advantage.
[3] Black will be hard put to hold his position, e.g. 13 . . . KN–Q4; 14 B–B5, R–K1; 15 R–K1, B–K3; 16 N–Q4, or 13 . . . B–K3; 14 BxB, PxB; 15 QxQ, KRxQ; 16 RxP! 16 . . . RxR; 17 BxN, KR–R1! 18 BxR, RxB; 19 N–K5, or 13 . . . QN–Q4; 14 B–B5, R–K1; 15 R–K1, RxR†; 16 QxR, P–QN3; 17 B–Q4, B–N2; 18 R–Q1, Q–K1; 19 B–K5. White's advantage is clear in all of these variations.

Nimzo-Indian Defense

	WHITE	BLACK
1	P-Q4	N-KB3
2	P-QB4	P-K3
3	N-QB3	B-N5
4	P-K3	P-B4
5	B-Q3	P-Q4
6	N-B3	O-O
7	O-O	N-B3
8	P-QR3	BxN
9	PxB	PxBP
10	BxP	Q-B2
11	B-N5	B-Q2
12	R-K1?[1]	....
	see diagram	
12	....	NxP!
13	NxN	PxN
14	BxB	PxKP!
15	B-R4[2]	PxP†
16	KxP	QxRP[3]

Black has a winning attack

BLACK TO PLAY
A most innocent-looking position. Black, however, by his next move shows that White's B-N5 was a mistake.

[1] Either 12 P–QR4! or 12 Q–K2 was indicated.

[2] Necessary, or White will be minus a Pawn without compensation.

[3] Black must win, as the White King is too exposed and there are threats of 17 . . . Q–R5† and 18 . . . N–N5 and/or KR–Q1. A likely continuation now would be 17 B–KN5 (to prevent 17 . . . Q–R5†), KR–Q1; 18 Q–B3, R–Q4 and Black must win.

	WHITE	BLACK
1	P-Q4	N-KB3
2	P-QB4	P-K3
3	N-QB3	B-N5
4	P-K3	P-B4
5	B-Q3	P-Q4
6	N-B3	O-O
7	O-O	N-B3
8	P-QR3	BxN
9	PxB	PxBP
10	BxP	Q-B2
11	B-Q3	P-K4
12	Q-B2	Q-K2
13	PxKP	NxP
14	NxN	QxN
15	P-KB4!	Q-K2[1]
16	P-B4	R-K1
17	R-K1	N-K5
18	B-N2	P-B3[2]

see diagram

| 19 | B-K5![3] | . . . . |

WHITE TO PLAY

Now White has an elegant move in hand that wins at least a Pawn in all variations. The move is quiet, sharp, and profound.

White has a winning advantage

[1] 15 . . . Q-R4 leads to more active counterplay, e.g. 16 P-B4 (if 16 P-K4, P-B5!; 17 B-K2, B-N5; 18 BxB, NxB; 19 P-R3, Q-B4† with fine play for Black), 16 . . . R-Q1; 17 P-K4, B-N5; 18 B-N2, RxB; 19 QxR, B-K7; 20 Q-N3, BxR; 21 RxB, Q-N3 and Black should be able to hold the ending.

[2] It is absolutely essential for Black to prevent P-K4-5, which (as so often in the Nimzoindian Defense) would yield White an overwhelming position.

[3] This neat move results in clear positional advantage for White. Black is advised to capture the Bishop and after 19 . . . PxB; 20 BxN, P-KN3 (the Rook Pawn must be protected, for after 20 . . . PxP; 21 PxP! and the threats of 22 BxP†, 22 B-Q5†, and 22 BxNP are more than poor Black can manage, and if 20 . . . P-KR3, White retains great advantage after either 21 B-Q5† followed by 22 Q-K4, or even 21 B-N6 and 22 Q-K4); 21 BxP is very promising, e.g. 21 . . . PxB; 22 QxP†, K-R1 (not 22 . . . K-B1; 23 PxP and 24 R-KB1†); 23 QR-Q1 and Black is hard put to find a move. The piece sacrifice with 21 BxP is not necessary to insure White's advantage as 21 B-Q5† and 22 Q-K4 leave White with a definite pull.

Nimzo-Indian Defense

	WHITE	BLACK
1	P-Q4	N-KB3
2	P-QB4	P-K3
3	N-QB3	B-N5
4	P-K3	P-B4
5	B-Q3	P-Q4
6	N-B3	O-O
7	O-O	N-B3
8	P-QR3	BxN
9	PxB	PxBP
10	BxP	Q-B2
11	B-Q3	P-K4
12	Q-B2	B-N5
13	NxP	NxN
14	PxN	QxP
15	P-B3	B-Q2
16	R-K1?[1]	....

see diagram

| 16 | .... | B-R5! |
| 17 | Q-N2[2] | QR-Q1[3] |

**Black has a sharp
positional edge**

BLACK TO PLAY

*Here Black has a chance to
decoy a White piece from defending a Pawn. Without
looking at the text continuation, can you spot Black's next
move, which will give him a
positional win?*

---

[1] White overlooks Black's clever reply. Here he should play 16 P–K4
with a good game.

[2] 17 QxB, QxP regains the piece and Black remains at least a Pawn
ahead.

[3] Now Black remains with a clear advantage, as White is unable to
contest the Queen file, owing to the strong placement of the Black
Bishop at R5. A likely variation now is 18 B–B1, P–QN3; 19 P–QB4,
KR–K1; 20 QxQ, RxQ; 21 P–K4, N–Q2; 22 B–N2, R–K3; 23 P–K5,
N–N1; 24 B–K2, N–B3 with excellent winning chances.

Nimzo-Indian Defense

	WHITE	BLACK
1	P-Q4	N-KB3
2	P-QB4	P-K3
3	N-QB3	B-N5
4	P-K3	P-B4
5	B-Q3	P-Q4
6	N-B3	O-O
7	O-O	N-B3
8	P-QR3	BxN
9	PxB	PxBP
10	BxP	Q-B2
11	B-Q3	P-K4
12	Q-B2	B-N5
13	NxP	NxN
14	PxN	QxP
15	P-R3?[1]	. . . .

see diagram

15	. . . .	QR-Q1
16	PxB[2]	NxP
17	BxPch[3]	K-R1
18	P-N3	P-KN3
19	P-QB4[4]	KxB
20	B-N2	Q-R4
21	P-B3	NxP
22	Q-B3	Q-R3![5]

**Black has positional
superiority**

BLACK TO PLAY

Black feels that fast development and dangerous attacking chances against White's undeveloped forces are worth the piece.

---

[1] Here 15 P-B3, striving for P-K4 and B-K3, is customary and certainly preferable to 15 P-R3.

[2] 15 B-N2 is much safer.

[3] If 17 P-KB4, Q-R4; 18 P-N3, RxB or 17 P-N3, RxB; 18 QxR, Q-R4. Both variations naturally win for Black.

[4] If 19 BxP, PxB; 20 QxP, R-KN1; 21 Q any, Q-R4 and Black wins.

[5] And not 22 . . . N-B4; 23 K-N2! However, after 22 . . . Q-R3 Black should win easily, e.g. 23 R-B2, N-Q8 or 23 KR-K1, N-B4 and Black has various threats such as 24 . . . R-Q7 or 24 . . . N-Q5 or 24 . . . NxP and he is a Pawn ahead to boot.

Nimzo-Indian Defense 73

	WHITE	BLACK
1	P-Q4	N-KB3
2	P-QB4	P-K3
3	N-QB3	B-N5
4	Q-B2	P-B4
5	PxP	O-O
6	B-N5	N-R3
7	P-QR3	BxN†
8	QxB	NxP
9	P-B3?[1]	KN-K5[2]
10	BxQ	NxQ
11	B-K7[3]	....

see diagram

| 11 | .... | N-N6[4] |
| 12 | BxR[5] | KxB![6] |

Black has all the winning chances

BLACK TO PLAY
Black has foreseen White's sortie with the Bishop. His surprise rejoinder 11 . . . N–N6 gives him a positional win against White's best resource.

---

[1] A weak move which saddles White with the inferior game. He fears 9 ... QN–K5 with possibilities of 10 . . . NxB or 10 . . . Q–R4†, and so he attempts to prevent an incursion on his K4. He should have played 9 BxN with approximate equality.

[2] Surprising but quite good. Black remains with the better chances in the endgame.

[3] If 11 PxN, RxB and White's weak Pawns should cost him the game. Now White is attacking a Rook and both Knights, yet Black's position is preferable.

[4] The pretty point which White overlooked.

[5] Again if 12 PxN, NxR; 13 BxR, KxB and the Black Knight escapes via N6. In this situation, the doubled QB Pawns must lose.

[6] Now in order to avoid the organic Pawn weaknesses, White must play 13 R–Q1, NxR; 14 KxN. After 14 . . . P–Q4 White has serious problems developing his remaining pieces, and Black will threaten to penetrate with his Rook on the Queen Bishop or Queen file. A bad and probably lost game for Black.

	WHITE	BLACK
1	P-Q4	N-KB3
2	P-QB4	P-K3
3	N-QB3	B-N5
4	P-QR3	BxN†
5	PxB	O-O
6	P-B3	P-Q4
7	PxP	PxP
8	P-K3	B-B4
9	N-K2	QN-Q2
10	N-B4	P-B4
11	B-Q3	BxB
12	QxB	R-K1
13	O-O	R-QB1
14	R-N1	Q-R4
15	RxP	N-N3[1]
16	P-N4	P-KR3?[2]
17	P-KR4	PxP
18	P-N5	PxKP[3]
19	PxN	RxP
	see diagram	
20	Q-N6	. . . .[4]

WHITE TO PLAY

White is convinced that it is profitable to give immediately and whole-heartedly. The Queen, "cast upon the waters", is returned with more than double profit.

Black cannot avoid checkmate

[1] This attempt at counterplay is ill-advised, since White not only gains a Pawn by capturing on N7, but his Rook develops great activity.

[2] This merely weakens the Black King position and does no good. 16 . . . PxP immediately was preferable.

[3] This attempt at counterplay fails because of the weakness of his own King position.

[4] Black can't defend against 21 QxP mate except by 20 . . . PxQ, when 21 RxP, followed by 22 N-N6 is mate.

Norris Gambit

WHITE	BLACK
1 P-Q4	P-Q4
2 B-B4	P-QB4
3 P-K4	N-QB3
4 N-QB3	PxQP
5 PxP	PxN
6 PxN	Q-R4
7 P-QN4	QxNP

see diagram

8 Q-Q5![1]	B-K3
9 Q-B3	0-0-0
10 PxP†[2]	....

White has an overwhelming attack

WHITE TO PLAY

White's diabolical reply to Black's last move offers a Bishop, permits his Queen to be assailed by an enemy Knight or Bishop. Despite these drawbacks, the move wins in all variations.

---

[1] The sockdolager. White threatens 9 PxP followed by B-N5†, and if 9 ... P-K3; 10 PxP! anyway.

[2] And White wins, e.g. 10 ... QxP; 11 B-QR6!, QxB; 12 Q-R8†, K-Q2; 13 R-Q1†.

	WHITE	BLACK
1	P-K4	P-K4
2	N-KB3	N-KB3
3	NxP	P-Q3
4	N-KB3	NxP
5	P-Q4	P-Q4
6	B-Q3	B-Q3
7	O-O	B-KN5
8	P-B4	O-O[1]
9	PxP	P-KB4
10	N-B3[2]	N-Q2
11	R-K1?	....

see diagram

BLACK TO PLAY

Here is the setting for a double fireworks display, leaving Black with two Pawns for the Exchange and a slight endgame edge.

11	....	BxP†!?[3]
12	KxB	NxP
13	B-KN5	NxQ[4]
14	BxQ	NxN[5]
15	B-K7	NxQP
16	BxR	RxB
17	N-K5[6]	N/2-B3

Black has a positional advantage

[1] Another of Marshall's tricky variations, whereby Black gambits material for attack.

[2] And not 10 R-K1?, BxP†!; 11 KxB, NxP; 12 Q-K2, NxB; 13 QxN, BxN; 14 QxB, Q-R5†; 15 Q-R3, QxR when Black has won the exchange.

[3] But now this brilliant conception is somewhat dubious.

[4] Or 13 ... QxB; 14 NxQ, BxQ; 15 QRxB, NxR; 16 NxN and White has two pieces for the Rook.

[5] 14 ... QRxB; 15 QRxN leaves White a piece ahead.

[6] Black's Pawns are sufficient compensation for the exchange though the win, if it exists, is very difficult.

Philidor's Defense

	WHITE	BLACK
1	P-K4	P-K4
2	N-KB3	P-Q3
3	P-Q4	N-KB3
4	N-B3	QN-Q2
5	B-QB4	B-K2
6	BxP†?[1]	KxB
7	N-N5†	K-N1[2]
8	N-K6	Q-K1
9	NxBP	Q-N3
10	NxR[3]	. . . .

see diagram

10	. . . .	QxP
11	R-B1	PxP
12	QxP	N-K4!
13	P-B4[4]	N/3-N5[5]

White must lose his Queen

BLACK TO PLAY

White will pay dearly for this Rook capture. This ancient opening must be handled with the utmost finesse by both sides in order to avoid the abundant traps, some of which boomerang.

---

[1] A tempting but unsound sacrifice. White calculates that he can force the win of the Black Queen's Rook but fails to appreciate the vigor of Black's counterplay.

[2] The only move. 7 . . . K–K1 or 7 . . . K–B1 costs the Queen after 8 N–K6 and 7 . . . K–N3; 8 P–KR4, P–KR4; 9 P–KB4, PxP; 10 N–K2 followed by 11 NxBP is lethal.

[3] White might put up some sort of fight with 10 O–O, though after 10 . . . R–N1 his two Pawns do not constitute adequate compensation for the piece.

[4] Hoping for 13 . . . N–B6†; 14 RxN, QxR; 15 Q–B4† winning the Bishop with check.

[5] The crusher. White has no satisfactory rejoinder to the threat of 14 . . . B–R5†. If 14 B–K3, B–R5†, 15 B–B2, N–B6† wins the Queen.

Philidor's Defense

	WHITE	BLACK
1	P-K4	P-K4
2	N-KB3	P-Q3
3	P-Q4	N-Q2
4	B-QB4	P-QB3
5	N-B3	B-K2
6	PxP	PxP[1]
7	N-KN5	N-R3[2]
	see diagram	
8	N-K6!	PxN
9	BxN	N-N3[3]
10	Q-R5†	K-B1
11	B-N3	PxB[4]
12	R-Q1	Q-K1
13	QxP†	K-B2
14	R-Q3	B-B3
15	R-B3	N-Q2[5]
16	P-N4	K-N1
17	P-N5[6]	. . . .

White wins decisive material

WHITE TO PLAY

The potency of White's continuation is based on the awkward position of the Black Knight at KR3 and the vulnerability of Black's KB2.

---

[1] Perhaps Black should try the recapture with the Knight, since White obtains a positional advantage after the text.

[2] After 7 . . . BxN; 8 Q–R5, P–KN3; 9 QxB or 8 . . . Q–B3; 9 BxB, Q–N3; 10 Q–R4, White has the two Bishops and a minimal positional edge, but the text is more dangerous.

[3] Not 9 . . . PxB; 10 Q–R5†, K–B1; 11 BxP, Q–K1; 12 QxP mate.

[4] 11 . . . B–B3, although in White's favor, offers better fighting chances.

[5] 15 . . . Q–K2 is also met by 6 P–N4 winning the pinned Bishop.

[6] All Black's Bishop or Queen moves are met incisively by 18 BxP†. Now White recaptures the sacrificed Bishop and remains with an overwhelming attack.

Philidor's Defense

	WHITE	BLACK
1	P-K4	P-K4
2	N-KB3	P-Q3
3	B-B4	B-K2
4	P-Q4	PxP[1]
5	NxP	N-Q2?[2]
	see diagram	
6	BxP†	KxB
7	N-K6	Q-K1[3]
8	NxBP	Q-Q1
9	Q-R5†[4]	P-N3
10	Q-Q5†	K-B3
11	B-N5†	K-N2
12	N-K6†	....[5]

**White wins both Queen
and King**

WHITE TO PLAY
*After four moves Black is
lost; in no other opening does
punishment follow so quickly
after a careless move as in
Philidor's Defense.*

[1] This ceding of the center gives Black's game too passive a character.
[2] And this is a blunder. 5 . . . N–KB3 and 6 . . . O–O was indicated.
[3] Or 7 . . . KxN; 8 Q–Q5†, K–B3; 9 Q–B5 mate.
[4] A subtle check, the purpose of which is to deny the Black King access to KN3.
[5] And White wins the Queen.

Philidor's Defense

	WHITE	BLACK
1	P-K4	P-K4
2	N-KB3	P-Q3
3	P-Q4	N-Q2
4	B-B4	P-QB3
5	O-O	B-K2
6	Q-K2	KN-B3
7	R-Q1	Q-B2
8	PxP	PxP?[1]
9	N-N5	O-O
	see diagram	
10	BxP†	RxB[2]
11	Q-B4[3]	. . . .

WHITE TO PLAY

Black has "developed" five pieces, while White has "developed" only four. The word "development", however, is a badly abused word. In this position it's evident that Black has erred badly—he has not placed the right pieces on the right squares.

White wins decisive material

[1] 8 . . . QNxP is playable and gives fair chances, e.g. 9 B–N3, B–N5.
[2] If 10 . . . K–R1; 11 N–K6 wins the exchange.
[3] White will capture the King Rook with an easy win in prospect.

Philidor's Defense

	WHITE	BLACK
1	P-K4	P-K4
2	N-KB3	P-Q3
3	P-Q4	N-KB3
4	PxP	NxP
5	B-QB4[1]	B-K3[2]
6	BxB	PxB
7	Q-K2[3]	P-Q4
8	Q-N5†[4]	N-B3
9	N-Q4	Q-Q2
10	QxNP?[5]	. . . .

see diagram

10	. . . .	B-N5†!
11	P-B3[6]	NxN!!
12	QxR†[7]	K-B2
13	QxR	Q-N4!![8]

Black cannot avoid checkmate

BLACK TO PLAY

White threatens QxR and NxN. Black's strong retort is a demonstration of spirit over matter.

---

[1] 5 QN–Q2 or 5 Q–Q5 offers a better chance for an advantage.

[2] 5 . . . P–QB3 is a simpler means of equalizing, but Black is not interested in simplicity.

[3] 7 O–O or 7 QN–Q2 gives White a good game.

[4] This time-wasting expedition is suspect.

[5] White continues his faulty plan.

[6] 11 . . . NxN!! is a good answer to *any* White 11th move.

[7] White's game is beyond redemption. 12 QxB, N–B7† or 12 O–O, O–O and Black, with an extra piece and the threat of . . . N–B7, wins easily.

[8] And White is powerless to prevent mate on his K2.

Philidor's Defense

	WHITE	BLACK
1	P-K4	P-K4
2	N-KB3	P-Q3
3	P-Q4	P-KB4?[1]
4	QPxP	BPxP
5	N-N5	P-Q4
6	N-QB3[2]	B-QN5
7	P-K6	BxN†?[3]
8	PxB	N-KR4[4]
	see diagram	
9	Q-R5†	K-B1[5]
10	B-R3†	K-N1
11	Q-B7†	NxQ
12	PxN	....

Black has been checkmated

WHITE TO PLAY

To checkmate your opponent with a Pawn is a rare privilege. Here, White has the chance to do so in five moves.

---

[1] A premature attacking move which results in a weakening of the King side.

[2] Immediately 6 P-K6 is stronger than the text move and should win for White.

[3] This loses. Black had chances with 7 ... P-Q5; 8 N-B7, Q-B3; 9 P-QR3, BxKP; 10 NxR, PxN.

[4] Otherwise 9 N-B7 wins the exchange, but 8 ... Q-B3; 9 N-B7, BxP would have been the lesser evil.

[5] 9 ... K-K2 is a little better, though White has his choice of several winning continuations, e.g. 10 N-B7 or 10 NxKP (threat 11 B-N5†) or 10 B-R3†, K-B3; 11 N-B7.

Pirc Defense

	WHITE	BLACK
1	P-Q4	N-KB3
2	N-KB3	P-Q3
3	N-B3	B-B4
4	N-KR4	B-N3
5	NxB	RPxN
6	P-K4	QN-Q2
7	B-QB4	P-K4
8	O-O	P-B3
9	P-QR4	PxP
10	QxP	N-N5
11	P-R3	N/2-K4!?[1]
	see diagram	
12	PxN?[2]	N-B6†
13	PxN	Q-R5[3]

White cannot avoid checkmate

BLACK TO PLAY

Black's following double Knight sacrifice is based on the blockade of all escape exits for the White King.

---

[1] Both sides have treated the opening in an original fashion. Objectively, White probably has a theoretical advantage; he has the two Bishops and a better hold on the center, but he must be very careful, as the Rook's file and Black's Knight can be extremely dangerous.

[2] This loses, as does 12 B-N3, RxP; 13 P-KB4 (if 13 PxR, N-B6† wins the Queen), R-R8†; 14 KxR, Q-R5†; 15 K-N1, Q-R7 mate. 12 B-K2 is good here.

[3] White is helpless to prevent mate at R8 and R7.

84 *Polish Opening*

	WHITE	BLACK
1	P-QN4	P-K4
2	B-N2	P-KB3
3	P-K4	BxP
4	B-B4	N-QB3[1]
5	P-B4	PxP
6	N-KR3!	KN-K2
7	NxP	N-R4[2]
	see diagram	
8	BxP!	R-B1[3]
9	N-R5	NxB[4]
10	NxP†	K-B2
11	O-O	K-N1
12	Q-R5!	RxB[5]
13	RxR	N-KN3
14	RxN	PxR
15	QxP	K-R1[6]
16	N-K8!	Q-K2
17	N-B6	. . . .[7]

Black cannot avoid checkmate

WHITE TO PLAY

An eccentric opening leads to an eccentric position. In attempting to destroy White's dangerous King Bishop, Black overlooks the dangerous stroke which this Bishop may deliver.

[1] Black would do better to play 4 . . . KN–K2 followed by 5 . . . P–Q4. As play progresses White obtains fine attacking chances.

[2] Black wishes to drive the White Bishop off the QR2–KN8 diagonal in order to be able to castle, but he is in for a rude shock.

[3] And not 8 . . . NxB (8 . . . PxB; 9 Q–R5† is even worse); 9 Q–R5†, K–B1 (9 . . . P–N3; 10 NxP!); 10 N–N6†, K–N1; 11 BxN, BxB (11 . . . PxN; 12 Q–Q5†); 12 Q–Q5 mate.

[4] Not 12 . . . PxB; 13 N–N7 mate.

[5] Forced; the Bishop is too strong.

[6] White threatened discovered check winning the Queen and 15 . . . N–K4; 16 Q–N3 wins the Knight.

[7] Black resigns for if 17 . . . Q–N2; 18 Q–R5† mates.

Queen's Fianchetto

	WHITE	BLACK
1	P-K4	P-QN3[1]
2	P-Q4	B-N2
3	N-QB3	P-K3
4	N-B3	N-KB3
5	B-Q3	P-B4
6	O-O	P-B5[2]
7	BxP	NxP
8	NxN	BxN
9	N-N5	B-N3
10	P-Q5	B-K2
	see diagram	
11	PxP!	BxN[3]
12	PxBP†	K-B1
13	BxB	QxB
14	Q-Q6†	Q-K2
15	KR-K1	....

**Black must lose his Queen
or be checkmated**

WHITE TO PLAY

White, ahead in space and development, can now penetrate Black's King-side defenses by a well-timed sacrificial continuation.

---

[1] Not recommended, as it gives White too free a hand in the center.

[2] Now 6 . . . PxP transposes into a form of the Sicilian, somewhat in White's favor. With 6 . . . P–B5 Black exchanges his Queen Bishop Pawn for White's King Pawn, but he loses valuable time in the process.

[3] If 11 . . . BPxP; 12 Q–B3, N–B3 (or 12 . . . P–Q4; 13 NxKP!) or 12 . . . N–R3; 13 NxKP! and 11 . . . QPxP; 12 Q–B3, N–Q2; 13 R–Q1, O–O; 14 NxKP, PxN; 15 BxP†, K–R1; 16 Q–N3 regaining the piece, and with two extra Pawns, White should win, though this is Black's best chance.

	WHITE	BLACK
1	P-Q4	P-Q4
2	P-QB4	PxP
3	N-KB3	P-QB4[1]
4	P-Q5	N-KB3?[2]
5	N-B3	P-K3
6	P-K4!	PxP
7	P-K5	P-Q5?[3]
	see diagram	
8	BxP![4]	N-B3?
9	PxN	PxN
10	Q-K2†	K-Q2[5]
11	B-B4!	Q-R4
12	R-Q1†	N-Q5
13	B-QN5†[6]	....

WHITE TO PLAY

Black expects a routine swap of Knights, overlooking the strength of White's next move which threatens to win the Queen.

White has an overwhelming attack

---

[1] A seldom seen move which generally transposes into better known variations if White replies with 4 P-K3.

[2] Here Black should play 4 ... P-K3 with an easy game after 5 P-K4, PxP; 6 PxP, N-KB3; 7 BxP, B-Q3.

[3] Black is better advised to try 7 ... N-K5 and if 8 NxP, Q-R4†, although White has the better ending if he plays simply 8 NxN, PxN; 9 QxQ†, KxQ; 10 N-N5, B-K3; 11 NxB†, PxN; 12 BxP.

[4] Very strong. The intention is to meet 8 ... PxN with 9 BxP†, K-K2 (or he loses the Queen); 10 PxN†, PxP; 11 Q-N3, Q-N3! (if 11 ... PxP; 12 O-O with a winning attack); 12 O-O, QxQ; 13 BxQ and Black's backward development and exposed King should make successful defense impossible. However, this variation offered better chances than 8 ... N-B3? Which leads to a rapid debacle.

[5] All interpositions cost a piece.

[6] Now if 13 ... K-Q1; 14 Q-K8 mates, so White wins the Queen and should mate quickly as well.

Queen's Gambit Accepted

	WHITE	BLACK
1	P-Q4	P-Q4
2	P-QB4	PxP
3	N-KB3	N-KB3
4	Q-R4†	QN-Q2
5	N-B3	P-K3
6	P-K4	P-B4
7	P-Q5	PxP
8	P-K5	P-Q5?[1]
9	BxP	PxN
10	PxN	QxP
11	B-KN5	Q-B3
	see diagram	
12	0-0-0[2]	....

White gains decisive material

WHITE TO PLAY

Black is sure that in White's hurry to develop all his pieces, he has overlooked his Queen. Has he?

---

[1] A serious mistake. Black should play 8 . . . P-QN4!; 9 QxNP, R-QN1; 10 Q-R4, P-Q5; 11 PxN, PxN; 12 BxP, R-N5! (not 12 . . . PxP; 13 BxP†, KxB; 14 N-N5† with a winning attack); 13 Q-Q1! and though White has a dangerous initiative, Black has chances of holding the balance.

[2] Black is helpless against the threat of 13 KR-K1†. He must try 12 . . . QxQ (if 12 . . . N-B3; 13 B-N5); 13 KR-K1†, B-K2 (13 . . . N-K4; 14 R-Q8 mate); 14 RxB†, K-B1 (if 14 . . . K-Q1; 15 R/7xN†, K-K1; 16 R-Q8 mate); 15 RxP†, K-N1 (if 15 . . . K-K1; 16 R-K1†, N-K4; 17 RxN†, B-K3; 18 BxB, PxP†; 19 KxP, Q-N5†; 20 B-N3 mate); 16 RxN†, QxB; 17 R-Q8†, K-B2; 18 N-K5† and White recovers the Queen, remains a piece ahead, and wins very easily.

	WHITE	BLACK
1	P-Q4	P-Q4
2	P-QB4	PxP
3	N-QB3[1]	P-QB3
4	P-K3	P-QN4
5	NxP?[2]	PxN
6	Q-B3[3]	Q-B2
7	QxR	B-N2
8	QxP	....
	see diagram	
8	....	P-K4!
9	P-Q5[4]	B-B4
10	P-Q6[5]	BxQP[6]

BLACK TO PLAY

White's Queen has reached a dead end. Does this presage the death of the Pale Lady?

Black wins decisive material

[1] The right move is 3 N–KB3.

[2] White combines to win the exchange only to find his Queen trapped in the finale. 5 P–QR4 would lead to the recapture of the gambit Pawn with about an equal game.

[3] White's point—or so he thinks.

[4] Now White becomes aware of the danger, but it is too late. The threat was 9 . . . N–QB3 and the Queen has no retreat. 9 P–Q5 is designed to prevent this.

[5] Again the Queen has no move.

[6] And White has no defense against the twin threats of 10 . . . B–B4 and 10 . . . N–QB3.

Queen's Gambit Accepted

	WHITE	BLACK
1	P-Q4	P-Q4
2	P-QB4	PxP
3	N-KB3	N-KB3
4	P-K3	P-K3
5	BxP	P-B4
6	O-O	PxP
7	PxP	N-B3
8	N-B3	P-QR3
9	Q-K2	NxP?[1]
10	NxN	QxN
11	R-Q1	Q-N5?[2]
	see diagram	
12	N-Q5[3]	....

White wins decisive material

WHITE TO PLAY

Black, a Pawn plus, hopes to swap Queens, if White moves his Queen; then simple development gives Black the edge. White's sharp coup turns the tables.

---

[1] 9 ... B-K2 or 9 ... P-QN4 should be played. The Pawn capture is too risky.

[2] Black should retire his Queen to R2, although his backward development makes his game very difficult to defend.

[3] This surprising move forces the win of material. White threatens 13 NxN† followed by 14 QxQ, as well as 13 N-B7†. Black therefore must play 12 ... QxQ; 13 N-B7† (the winning *zwischenzug*), ... K-K2; 14 BxQ, R-N1 (if 14 ... R-R2; 15 B-K3, P-QN3; 16 BxP, R-N2; 17 B-B5 mate); 15 B-B4 and Black cannot meet White's diverse threats of 16 N-Q5†, 16 NxKP, 16 NxRP, 16 B-Q6† followed by 17 BxB† and 18 BxNP or 18 B-Q6† without yielding at least the exchange.

Queen's Gambit Accepted

	WHITE	BLACK
1	N-KB3	P-Q4
2	P-B4	PxP
3	P-K3	P-QB4
4	BxP	N-QB3
5	P-Q4	P-K3
6	O-O	N-B3
7	Q-K2	P-QR3
8	N-B3	P-QN4
9	B-N3	B-N2
10	R-Q1	Q-B2
11	P-Q5!	PxP
12	P-K4	PxP?[1]
13	NxP	NxN
14	QxN†	N-K2[2]
	see diagram	
15	BxP†	. . . .[3]

White mates shortly

WHITE TO PLAY

White now has an opportunity to finish Black off by a cute combination.

---

[1] Black should try 12 . . . O-O-O with an exciting game in prospect.

[2] Or 14 . . . B-K2; 15 B-B4 and if 15 . . . N-Q5; 16 QxN wins a piece, and 15 . . . Q-B1; 16 B-Q5, N-Q1 17 B-Q6 is decisive. If 14 . . . Q-K2; 15 Q-KB4, N-Q1; 16 R-K1, N-K3; 17 Q-KN4, P-B5; 18 B-N5! Q-B2; 19 RxN†, PxR; 20 QxP†, B-K2; 21 R-K1, winning easily.

[3] After 15 . . . KxB; 16 N-N5†, K-K1 (if 16 . . . K-N1; or 16 . . . K-B3; 17 Q-K6 mates); 17 Q-K7, Black cannot prevent the mate at KB7.

Queen's Gambit Declined

	WHITE	BLACK
1	P-Q4	P-Q4
2	P-QB4	P-K3
3	N-KB3	N-KB3
4	B-N5	B-N5†
5	N-B3	PxP
6	P-K4	P-B4
7	P-K5	PxP
8	Q-R4†	N-B3
9	O-O-O	B-Q2
10	N-K4	B-K2
11	PxN	PxP
12	B-R4	QR-B1
13	K-N1[1]	P-N4[2]
14	QxNP	P-B6
15	NxQP	P-QR3[3]
16	Q-N3	N-R4
17	Q-B2	PxP
18	QxP	B-B3
	see diagram	
19	B-QN5[4]	....

In the myriad variations ensuing, White will always maintain superiority

WHITE TO PLAY

It appears that Black has the more potent threats because of White's undefended Queen's Rook. But White is advantageously prepared to sacrifice a piece.

---

[1] An interesting and well-known position where the chances have always been assessed as roughly equal; Black's strong Pawns are about an equivalent for the extra piece.

[2] 13 . . . N–R4; 14 Q–B2, P–K4! also gives about equal chances.

[3] And not 15 . . . NxN; 16 RxN, BxQ; 17 BxB†, K–B1; 18 RxQ† and White should win. Also 15 . . . N–N5; 16 QxN!, BxQ; 17 NxP†, K–B1; 18 N–B2! is in White's favor.

[4] This fine move finally sets off White's advantage. Now 19 . . . BxB; 20 NxB, and 21 N(5)–Q6† will be murderous. Or 19 . . . PxB; 20 NxB, followed by 21 NxB and 22 BxP(†), is equally lethal.

BLACK TO PLAY

White's last move was a not-obvious blunder. Black has a winning refutation ready.

	WHITE	BLACK
1	P-Q4	P-Q4
2	P-QB4	P-K3
3	N-QB3	N-KB3
4	B-N5	QN-Q2
5	PxP	PxP
6	P-K3	B-K2
7	Q-B2	P-B3
8	B-Q3	O-O
9	N-B3	R-K1
10	O-O	N-B1
11	QR-N1	N-K5
12	BxB	QxB
13	P-QN4	P-QR3
14	P-QR4	N-N3
15	P-N5	RPxP
16	PxP	B-N5[1]
17	N-Q2?[2]	....

see diagram

| 17 | .... | NxN/7 |
| 18 | QxN | N-R5[3] |

Black must gain material

---

[1] The position is a typical one arising from the Exchange Variation of the Queen's Gambit Declined. While White pursues his operations on the Queen-side, Black strives for counterplay by means of a King-side attack.

[2] This plausible move loses at least a Pawn. Either 17 B-K2 or 17 BxN were preferable alternatives.

[3] White must now yield at least a Pawn in order to avert immediate disaster, e.g. 19 B-K2, B-R6!; 20 PxB, R-N4†; 21 B-N4, N-B6†, or 19 KR-K1, B-R6; 20 B-B1, Q-N4; 21 P-B4, N-B6†; 22 K-B2, NxQ; 23 PxQ, NxR or 19 K-R1, N-B6; 20 Q-B2, Q-R5; 21 P-R3 (or 21 PxN, BxP†; 22 K-N1, Q-N5 mate); 21 . . . BxP; 22 PxN, B-N5†; 23 K-N2 (or 23 K-R1, BxP followed by 24 . . . Q-R8 mate), 23 . . . Q-R6†; 24 K-N1, BxP and mate is unavoidable. Comparatively best is 19 P-B3, QxP†; 20 QxQ (if 20 R-B2, BxP! wins another Pawn) . . . RxQ; 21 KR-Q1 and Black is a Pawn ahead and should win.

	WHITE	BLACK
1	P-Q4	P-Q4
2	P-QB4	P-QB3
3	N-KB3	N-B3
4	N-B3	PxP
5	P-QR4	B-B4
6	N-K5	P-B4?[1]
7	P-K4!	NxP[2]
8	Q-B3	PxP?[3]
9	QxB	N-Q3
	see diagram	
10	BxP!![4]	P-K3
11	B-N5†[5]	K-K2
12	N-Q5†	PxN
13	N-N6†	....

White mates next move

WHITE TO PLAY

Seemingly, Black regains the piece with a good game, but White brilliantly refutes this idea.

---

[1] 6 ... P-K3 and if 7 P-B3, B-QN5; 8 P-K4, BxP; 9 PxB, NxP should be played.

[2] Other moves are no better, e.g. 7 ... PxP; 8 PxB, PxN; 9 QxQ†, KxQ; 10 NxP† or 7 ... BxP; 8 NxB, NxN; 9 Q-B3, N-Q3; 10 BxP (now the threat is 11 QxP†, NxQ; 12 BxN mate!), P-K3; 11 B-N5†, K-K2 (if a Knight interposes, White wins a piece); 12 PxP, NxB; 13 NxP mate.

[3] Black is already lost as the following shows: 8 ... NxN; 9 QxB, P-B3; 10 BxP! (10 ... PxN allows 11 B-B7 mate) or 8 ... N-Q3; 9 PxP wins a piece.

[4] Now if Black captures White's Queen or Bishop, White will mate at KB7.

[5] This is decisive, for if 11 ... N-Q2; 12 BxN†, QxB; 13 Q-B4 or 13 Q-N4 or 13 Q-Q3 leaves White a full piece ahead.

	WHITE	BLACK
1	P-Q4	P-Q4
2	N-KB3	N-KB3
3	P-B4	P-B3
4	PxP	PxP
5	N-B3	N-B3
6	B-B4	P-QR3[1]
7	P-K3	B-B4
8	N-K5	R-B1[2]
9	Q-N3	N-QR4[3]
10	Q-R4†	N-B3[4]
11	NxN	RxN
	see diagram	
12	BxP![5]	. . . .

WHITE TO PLAY

It seems that Black has solved the problem of how to develop his problem piece, the Queen Bishop. White proves, how-that Black has mishandled the opening.

White wins at least a Pawn with positional initiative

[1] This is a little too elaborate. Safest is 6 . . . P-K3 and another equalizing line is 6 . . . B-B4; 7 P-K3, P-K3; 8 Q-N3, B-N5!

[2] Better is 8 . . . P-K3 and if 9 Q-N3, B-K2! Then 10 QxNP?, N-R4 and the Queen has no retreat. However, after 8 . . . P-K3 White could try 9 P-KN4 and 10 P-KR4 with great complications.

[3] It is difficult to defend the NP and if 9 . . . P-QN4; 10 P-QR4 and the Black Rook Pawn is also vulnerable.

[4] If Black interposes at his Q2, White wins the Queen's Pawn.

[5] White has won a Pawn with an overwhelming position, as he threatens both 13 BxP and 13 B-QN5.

WHITE	BLACK
1 P–Q4	N–KB3
2 P–QB4	P–K3
3 N–KB3	P–Q4
4 B–N5	P–KR3
5 BxN	QxB
6 N–B3	B–N5
7 Q–N3	N–B3[1]
8 P–QR3	B–R4
9 P–K3	O–O
10 B–Q3[2]	P–K4![3]
11 BPxP	PxP
12 PxP[4]	R–K1†
13 K–B1[5]	. . . .

see diagram

13	QxN!!
14 PxQ	B–R6†
15 K–N1	NxP
16 Q–Q1	R–K8†
17 QxR[6]	NxP

White has been
checkmated

BLACK TO PLAY

Black can easily regain his Pawn, but he's out for bigger game and cannot be stopped.

---

[1] 7 . . . P–B4 is more usual. As the play progresses, Black repeatedly offers his Queen Pawn for attack and development, but White will have none of it.

[2] 10 PxP, PxP; 11 B–K2 leaves White with pressure on the Queen and Queen Knight Pawn and he would stand better.

[3] Now the game is opened up to Black's advantage.

[4] 12 PxN, PxN (threatening 13 . . . PxP†) is in Black's favor.

[5] 13 B–K2, RxB†; 14 KxR, QxN†; 15 KxQ, NxP† and 16 . . . NxQ.

[6] or 17 B–B1, RxB†; 18 QxR, NxP mate.

Queen's Gambit Declined

	WHITE	BLACK
1	P-Q4	P-Q4
2	P-QB4	P-QB4
3	N-KB3	QPxP
4	N-B3	PxP[1]
5	QxP	QxQ[2]
6	NxQ	P-QR3[3]
7	N-Q5	K-Q1
8	B-Q2	N-Q2[4]
	see diagram	
9	B-R5†	P-N3
10	N-B6†	K-K1
11	N-B7	....

Black has been checkmated

WHITE TO PLAY

Black has won a Pawn and swapped Queens. Usually, this is more than enough for equality in the opening. White's next move turns a true light on the picture.

---

[1] 4 ... P-K3 is safer.

[2] And the exchange of Queens leaves Black dangerously behind in development. Better was 5 ... B-Q2 and 6 ... N-QB3.

[3] White threatened 7 N/4-N5 with awkward consequences, but this cure is worse than the disease.

[4] White threatened 9 B-R5† and 10 N-B7† or 10 N-N6†, and 8 ... N-B3 is met by 9 NxN†, PxN; 10 B-R5†.

	WHITE	BLACK
1	P-Q4	P-Q4
2	P-QB4	P-QB4
3	BPxP	N-KB3
4	PxP	QxP
5	QxQ	NxQ
6	P-K4	N-N5
7	N-QR3	P-K4
8	B-K3	P-QR3?[1]
9	N-B3	P-B3
10	N-Q2	B-K3
11	B-QB4	BxB
12	N/2xB	BxP[2]
13	BxB	N-Q6†
14	K-K2	NxB

see diagram

15	N-N6	R-R2
16	QR-B1[3]	. . . .

**White wins decisive
material**

WHITE TO PLAY

*The longest way around is the
shortest way home here.
White will begin an attack on
Black's King Rook by first attacking Black's Queen Rook.*

[1] This mistake creates great difficulties for Black. Correct was 8 . . .
QN-R3; 9 BxN, NxB; 10 N-N5, B-Q2; 11 N-Q6†, BxN; 12 PxB,
B-B3; 13 P-B3, K-Q2; 14 R-Q1, KR-Q1 and Black should be able to
recapture the Pawn with . . . K-K3 and . . . RxP with equality.
[2] So Black recaptures the Pawn, but his backward development leaves
him prey to White's counterattack.
[3] White wins a piece, e.g. 16 . . . N/1-Q2; 17 NxN, NxN; 18 R-B8† or
16 . . . N-K3; 17 R-B8†, or 16 . . . N/4-Q2; 17 R-B8†.

Queen's Indian Defense

	WHITE	BLACK
1	P-Q4	N-KB3
2	P-QB4	P-QN3[1]
3	N-QB3	P-K3
4	P-K4	B-N5
5	P-K5	N-K5
6	Q-N4[2]	NxN
7	PxN	BxP†
8	K-Q1	K-B1[3]
9	R-N1	N-B3
	see diagram	
10	B-R3†	K-N1[4]
11	R-N3	BxP
12	QxP†[5]	KxQ
13	R-N3†	K-R3
14	B-B1†	K-R4[6]
15	B-K2†	K-R5
16	R-R3	. . . .

Black has been checkmated

WHITE TO PLAY

Willy-nilly, the Black King will undergo a long journey, but in any case he will survive longer than the White Queen.

---

[1] The immediate fianchetto is inferior as it allows White to build a strong Pawn center.

[2] A very promising Pawn sacrifice which Black is compelled to accept.

[3] 8 . . . BxR loses to 9 QxP, R-B1; 10 B-N5, P-KB3; 11 B-K2, Q-K2 (the threat was 12 B-R5†, and 11 . . . R-B2; 12 B-R5, Q-K2; 13 Q-N8†, Q-B1; 14 BxR†, K-K2 or K-Q1 15 BxP mate); 12 B-R5†, K-Q1 (here 12 . . . R-B2 transposes to the previous parenthetical note); 13 PxP and now 13 . . . QxQ; 14 PxQ†, R-B3; 15 BxR mate or 13 . . . Q-B2; 14 QxR†, QxQ; 15 P-B7†, Q-K2; 16 P-B8=Q mate or 13 . . . Q anywhere else; 14 P-B7†, Q-K2; 15 QxR mate.

[4] If 10 . . . P-Q3 or 10 . . . N-K2, 11 Q-B3 wins a piece.

[5] This forces mate.

[6] 14 . . . Q-N4; 15 BxQ†, K-R4 (if 15 . . . K-N2; 16 B-K7 mate and 15 . . . K-N3; 16 B-B6† K-R3; 17 B-N7†, K-R4; 18 B-K2†, K-R5; 19 B-B6 mate); 16 B-K2†, K-N3; 17 B-B6†, K-B4 (17 . . . K-R3; 18 B-N7 mate); 18 B-Q3†, K-B5; 19 Knight mates at K2 or R3.

Queen's Indian Defense

	WHITE	BLACK
1	P-Q4	N-KB3
2	N-KB3	P-QN3
3	P-KN3	B-N2
4	B-N2	P-N3[1]
5	O-O	B-N2
6	P-B4	O-O
7	N-B3	P-Q3
8	Q-B2	QN-Q2
9	R-Q1	R-K1
10	P-K4	P-K4
11	PxP	PxP
12	B-N5	P-B3[2]

see diagram

13	BxN	BxB
14	B-R3	R-K2[3]
15	R-Q6	Q-B2
16	QR-Q1	R-Q1
17	Q-Q2	B-B1
18	RxB!	....[4]

**White wins decisive
material**

WHITE TO PLAY
Now Black's attempt to retain the "strong point" center will be repulsed because of the fatal position of his Knights.

[1] The double fianchetto seldom works well for Black, who is unable to get his fair share of the central squares or files. Better is simply 4 . . . P-K3.

[2] Otherwise White will occupy Q5 with his Knight, but now the Bishop at QN2 makes a sad impression; moreover, White has a strong series of moves. Comparatively best was 12 . . . Q-K2.

[3] No better was 14 . . B-B1; 15 R-Q6, Q-B2; 16 QR-Q1! (but not 16 BxN, BxB; 17 RxB/6, K-N2!); 16 . . . R-K2 or 16 . . . R-Q1; 17 QR-Q1 winning a piece.

[4] White wins a piece and the game.

100   *Queen's Indian Defense*

	WHITE	BLACK
1	P-Q4	N-KB3
2	P-QB4	P-QN3
3	P-KB3?	P-K3
4	P-Q5[1]	B-N5†
5	N-Q2	O-O
6	P-K4?[2]	PxP
7	BPxP	....
	see diagram	
7	....	NxKP
8	PxN	Q-R5†
9	K-K2[3]	B-R3†
10	K-B3	P-KB4[4]

BLACK TO PLAY

White's Pawn front has an imposing air, but Black shows up its basic weakness.

White will be checkmated in a few moves or lose his Queen

[1] 4 P-K4 is quite good for White here, as 4 ... NxP is unsound. White should plan on playing P-Q5 in answer to a Black ... P-QB4.

[2] Now this allows a sound sacrifice. 6 Q-N3 was preferable.

[3] 9 P-N3, QxKP† wins the King Rook.

[4] Black threatens 11 ... PxP† as well as 11 ... Q-N5† winning the Queen. White is helpless.

Queen's Indian Defense

	WHITE	BLACK
1	P-Q4	N-KB3
2	P-QB4	P-K3
3	N-KB3	P-QN3
4	P-KN3	B-N2
5	B-N2	P-B4
6	P-Q5	PxP
7	N-R4	P-Q3
8	N-QB3	Q-Q2
9	NxP	NxN
10	BxN	B-K2[1]
11	N-B5!	0-0
	see diagram	
12	BxB	QxB
13	Q-Q5![2]	. . . .

White gains decisive material

WHITE TO PLAY
Black will lose because of the insecure position of his Queen Rook. Can you see why?

---

[1] A serious mistake. 10 . . . N–B3 should be played, and though White has some advantage, there is no forced win.

[2] If 13 . . . QxQ; 14 NxB†, K–R1; 15 NxQ, and if 13 . . . N–B3; 14 NxB† (or 14 QxN) wins a piece.

Queen Pawn Game

	WHITE	BLACK
1	P-Q4	P-Q4
2	P-QB4	N-QB3
3	PxP	QxP
4	N-KB3	B-N5¹
5	N-B3	Q-QR4²
6	P-Q5	O-O-O
7	B-Q2	BxN
8	KPxB	N-N5?³
	see diagram	
9	P-QR3	NxP⁴
10	N-R4!!⁵	. . . .

WHITE TO PLAY

Black threatens to win a Pawn. How does White prevent this? Or does he?

White wins decisive material

---

¹ Black should play 4 . . . P-K4 and then 5 PxP, QxQ†; 6 KxQ, B-KN5; 7 B-B4, O-O-O†, followed by 8 . . . KN-K2 and 9 . . . N-N3 with splendid possibilities.

² 5 . . . Q-Q1 is safer.

³ 8 . . . N-K4 or 8 . . . N-N1 offers better possibilities of defense, although White retains fine attacking chances against Black's King and Queen with 9 R-B1.

⁴ This loses at least a piece. 9 . . . N-QR3 was certainly better, though White with 10 P-QN4 and 11 B-K3 or 10 N-N5 and 11 B-K3 has a winning attack.

⁵ Now Black's Queen is trapped and he must play 10 . . . N-N5 or 10 . . . N-B6, sacrificing the Knight in order to rescue her. Moreover, White still maintains a virulent attack.

	WHITE	BLACK
1	P-Q4	N-KB3
2	B-N5	P-Q4
3	N-Q2	P-K3
4	P-K3	B-K2
5	KN-B3	QN-Q2
6	B-Q3	P-B4
7	P-B3	P-QN3
8	Q-R4	O-O
9	N-K5	NxN?[1]
10	PxN	N-Q2[2]

see diagram

| 11 | Q-R4 | . . . . |

White wins material

WHITE TO PLAY

White's dark-square Bishop is attacked by Black's dark-square Bishop. Instead of defending his Bishop, White attacks the attacking Bishop!

[1] After 9 . . . B-N2, White can get the two Bishops by 10 N-B6, but Black's position would be satisfactory. The text, surprisingly enough, loses by force.

[2] There is only one variation to save the piece, e.g. not 10 . . . N-K1; 11 Q-R4 nor 10 . . . N-R4; 11 BxB, QxB; 12 P-KN4, nor again 10 . . . N-K5; 11 BxB, QxB; 12 NxN, PxN; 13 QxP winning the Queen Rook, nor 10 . . . P-B5; 11 PxN, PxP; 12 B-R6, PxB; 13 Q-N4†, K-R1; 14 Q-N7 mate. Only 10 . . . N-K5; 11 BxB, QxB; 12 NxN, P-B5! allows Black to save the piece, and even here White will be one or two Pawns ahead with a theoretical win.

Queen Pawn Game

	WHITE	BLACK
1	P-Q4	P-Q4
2	N-KB3	N-KB3
3	P-K3	P-B4
4	P-B3	P-K3
5	B-Q3	B-Q3
6	QN-Q2	QN-Q2
7	O-O	O-O
8	R-K1	R-K1
9	P-K4	QPxP
10	NxP	NxN
11	BxN	PxP
	see diagram	
12	BxP†[1]	KxB
13	N-N5†	K-N3
14	P-KR4	R-R1
15	RxP†[2]	N-B3
16	P-R5†	K-R3
17	RxB	Q-R4
18	NxP†	K-R2
19	N-N5†	K-N1
20	Q-N3†[3]	. . . .

Black can't avoid mate

WHITE TO PLAY

If White takes the Queen Pawn he has no more than an even game. But by capturing some other Pawn (which one?) he wins the game.

---

[1] This sacrifice is standard in positions of this type.

[2] This second sacrifice, which cannot be accepted, is the key to the Black King position. If 15 . . . PxR; 16 P-R5†, RxP; 17 Q-Q3†, K-B3; 18 Q-B3†, K-N3; (18 . . . K-K4; 19 Q-K4†, K-B3; 20 QxKP mate.) 19 Q-B7†, K-R3; 20 NxP†, K-R2; 21 QxP mate.

[3] And mates shortly.

Ruy Lopez

	WHITE	BLACK
1	P-K4	P-K4
2	N-KB3	N-QB3
3	B-N5	P-Q3
4	P-Q4	PxP
5	QxP	B-Q2
6	BxN	BxB
7	N-QB3	N-KB3
8	B-N5	B-K2
9	O-O-O	O-O
10	P-KR4	P-KR3
	see diagram	
11	N-Q5!	PxB[1]
12	NxB†	QxN
13	PxP	NxP
14	R-R5	Q-K3
15	QR-R1	P-B4
16	N-K5![2]	PxN[3]
17	P-N6[4]	....

White forces mate

WHITE TO PLAY

White's Queen Bishop is attacked. Should he retreat it, or capture Black's Knight? Or is there still another continuation?

---

[1] The acceptance of the sacrifice meets with a subtle refutation. Black should play 11 ... BxN and 12 ... R-K1 with fair chances for equality.

[2] Wins, for 16 ... QxN; 17 QxQ, PxQ; 18 P-N6 and mate at R8 cannot be averted.

[3] Or 16 ... P-KN3; 17 R-R8†, K-N2; 18 R(1)-R7 mate.

[4] Now 17 ... QxP; 18 Q-B4† and when Black interposes on B2, White plays R-R8 mate.

106

	WHITE	BLACK
1	P-K4	P-K4
2	N-KB3	N-QB3
3	B-N5	P-QR3
4	B-R4	P-Q3
5	P-Q4	P-QN4
6	B-N3	NxP
7	NxN	PxN
8	P-QB3	P-Q6?[1]
	see diagram	
9	P-QR4!	B-Q2?[2]
10	PxP	PxP?[3]
11	Q-R5![4]	Resigns

WHITE TO PLAY

Black's last move avoided the accelerated reply by White, 9 NxP, but White has an innocent-looking maneuver in reserve.

Black will be checkmated or lose decisive material

---

[1] Either 8 . . . B-N2 or 8 . . . PxP is preferable. After 8 . . . PxP White can either continue 9 NxP with some compensation for the Pawn minus, or he can force a draw with 9 Q-Q5, B-K3; 10 Q-B6†, B-Q2; 11 Q-Q5 and draws by repetition of moves.

[2] 9 . . . B-N2 should be played.

[3] 10 . . . BxP is the last chance to defend.

[4] Black is without defense against the mate at KB7 because of the vulnerability of his Queen Rook, e.g. 11 . . . P-N3; 12 Q-Q5, etc.

Ruy Lopez

	WHITE	BLACK
1	P-K4	P-K4
2	N-KB3	N-QB3
3	B-N5	P-QR3
4	B-R4	N-B3
5	N-B3	P-Q3
6	P-Q4[1]	P-QN4
7	B-N3[2]	PxP
8	NxQP[3]	NxN
9	QxN	....
	see diagram	
9	....	P-B4
10	Q-any	P-B5

Black has won a piece

BLACK TO PLAY
White dominates the center, but Black's Queen-side Pawns spring to life.

[1] If White intends to play P–Q4, he should preface it with 6 BxN†, PxB; 7 P–Q4.
[2] And if White suspected the danger, he could still play 7 PxP with about an even game.
[3] White's last chance to avoid losing a piece was with 8 B–Q5, NxB; 9 NxN, and the Pawn will soon be regained.

108

	WHITE	BLACK
1	P-K4	P-K4
2	N-KB3	N-QB3
3	B-N5	P-QR3
4	B-R4	N-B3
5	O-O	P-Q3
6	R-K1	P-QN4
7	B-N3	N-QR4
8	P-Q4	PxP[1]
	see diagram	
9	P-K5	PxP
10	NxKP	B-K3[2]
11	NxP	KxN
12	BxB†[3]	

WHITE TO PLAY

White will lose if he captures the Queen's Pawn, so he offers another Pawn instead; its capture, which can hardly be avoided, loses for Black.

White gains overwhelming material

---

[1] This loses. Black should try 8 . . . NxB; 9 PxN, B–N2 or 9 . . . N–Q2, and though White has somewhat better play, there are still chances for both sides.

[2] There is no better defense to the threat of 11 N–B6† and 11 NxP.

[3] Black must play 12 . . . K–K1 when 13 B–Q5† leaves White the exchange and a Pawn ahead with an easy win. If Black attempts to avoid this by 12 . . . K–N3 he will be mated as follows: 13 Q–Q3†, N–K5 (or 13 . . . K–R4; 14 Q–R3† and 15 Q–B5 mate); 14 QxN†, K–B3; 15 Q–R4†, K–N3; 16 Q–N4†, K–B3; 17 Q–N5 mate.

Ruy Lopez

	WHITE	BLACK
1	P-K4	P-K4
2	N-KB3	N-QB3
3	B-N5	P-QR3
4	B-R4	N-B3
5	P-Q3	P-Q3
6	P-B3	B-K2
7	QN-Q2	O-O
8	N-B1	P-QN4
9	B-B2	N-KR4
10	NxP?[1]	. . . .

see diagram

10	. . . .	NxN
11	QxN	B-N5[2]

White's Queen is lost

BLACK TO PLAY

Now follows a drama in three acts. 1. White wins a Pawn. 2. Greed cometh before a fall. 3. The trapper is trapped.

---

[1] Until now White has adopted a mode of play favored by Wilhelm Steinitz. This move is a blunder. Instead, he should play 10 N–N3 with a good position.

[2] And the White Queen is trapped. Black has looked ahead one move further than White.

	WHITE	BLACK
1	P-K4	P-K4
2	N-KB3	N-QB3
3	B-N5	P-QR3
4	BxN	QPxB
5	N-B3	P-B3
6	P-Q3	B-KN5
7	P-KR3	B-R4
8	B-K3	Q-Q2?[1]
	see diagram	
9	NxP	BxQ[2]
10	NxQ	BxP?[3]
11	NxB	KxN
12	K-Q2	. . . .[4]

White remains a piece to the good

WHITE TO PLAY

Black's last move was a mistake which permits White to win a Pawn. Black, anxious to regain the Pawn, loses to a zwischenzug (intermediary move) 10 BxP.

[1] Careless play which loses a Pawn. 8 . . . B-Q3 gives Black a satisfactory position.

[2] 9 . . . PxN; 10 QxB† is even worse for Black.

[3] And here Black should play 10 . . . KxN or 10 . . . B-R4, reconciling himself to the loss of a Pawn.

[4] The Bishop is trapped.

	WHITE	BLACK
1	P-K4	P-K4
2	N-KB3	N-QB3
3	B-N5	P-Q3
4	P-Q4	B-Q2
5	N-B3	N-B3
6	O-O	B-K2
7	R-K1	O-O?[1]
8	BxN	BxB
9	PxP	PxP
10	QxQ	QRxQ[2]
11	NxP	BxP[3]
12	NxB	NxN

see diagram

13	N-Q3[4]	P-KB4
14	P-KB3	B-B4†
15	NxB	NxN
16	B-N5	R-Q4[5]
17	B-K7	R-K1
18	P-QB4	RxB[6]
19	RxR	....

White wins at least the Exchange

WHITE TO PLAY

At first sight it seems that Black has weathered the opening storm. But White has a final winning coup.

[1] This loses at least a Pawn; Black outcombines himself.

[2] 10 ... KRxQ is no better, e.g. 11 NxP, BxP; 12 NxB, NxN; 13 N-Q3, P-KB4; 14 P-KB3, B-B4†; 15 K-B1, R-KB1 (to meet 16 PxN with 16 ... PxP† regaining the Knight); 16 K-K2, B-N3; 17 PxN, PxP; 18 N-B4, P-N4; 19 N-R3, P-N5; 20 N-B4 and White is a piece ahead.

[3] Not 11 ... NxP?; 12 NxB, NxN; 13 NxB†, K-R1; 14 PxN.

[4] Black hoped for 13 RxN?, R-Q8† and mate.

[5] Or 16 ... QR-K1; 17 B-K7 wins the exchange.

[6] If the other Rook moves, White has 19 BxN. Now White is the exchange ahead with a simple win in prospect.

Ruy Lopez

	WHITE	BLACK
1	P-K4	P-K4
2	N-KB3	N-QB3
3	B-N5	P-QR3
4	B-R4	N-B3
5	Q-K2	P-QN4
6	B-N3	B-K2
7	P-B3	O-O
8	O-O	P-Q4!?[1]
9	PxP	NxP
10	NxP	N-B5
11	Q-K4	NxN
12	QxR?[2]	....

see diagram

12	....	Q-Q6
13	B-Q1[3]	B-KR6
14	QxP	BxP
15	R-K1	Q-B6
16	BxQ[4]	NxB

White has been checkmated

BLACK TO PLAY

White has won the Exchange, but his backward development and the absence of his Queen from the battleground will destroy him.

---

[1] This sacrifice offers Black excellent attacking chances at the expense of a Pawn.

[2] It is more important for White to free his game at this time than to play for material gain. Correct is 12 P-Q4!

[3] Necessary, as Black was threatening 13 ... N-K7†; 14 K-R1, N-N6†; 15 RPxN, QxR†; 16 K-R2, N-N5†; 17 K-R3, Q-R8 mate.

[4] The threat was 16 ... N-R6 mate. 16 P-KR4 is likewise unavailing as 16 ... N-R6†; 17 K-R2, N-N5 is mate.

Ruy Lopez

	WHITE	BLACK
1	P-K4	P-K4
2	N-KB3	N-QB3
3	B-N5	P-QR3
4	B-R4	N-B3
5	O-O	B-K2
6	Q-K2	O-O?[1]
7	BxN	QPxB
8	NxP	Q-Q5[2]
9	N-KB3	QxKP?[3]
10	QxQ	NxQ
	see diagram	
11	R-K1[4]	....

**White wins decisive
material**

WHITE TO PLAY
*Black has the two-Bishop edge
and seemingly the better
chances, but White has ready
a winning one-step.*

[1] This loses at least a Pawn. 6 ... P-QN4 or 6 ... P-Q3 are usual in
this position.
[2] Black has counted heavily on this move to recover the Pawn. Simply
8 ... R-K1 offers better fighting chances.
[3] And so he recaptures the Pawn.
[4] To find he must lose a piece after 11 ... P-KB4; 12 P-Q3 and if the
Knight moves, 13 RxB.

114

	WHITE	BLACK
1	P-K4	P-K4
2	N-KB3	N-QB3
3	B-N5	P-QR3
4	B-R4	N-B3
5	O-O	P-Q3
6	Q-K2	P-QN4
7	B-N3	N-QR4
8	P-Q4	B-N5[1]
9	PxP	NxB[2]
10	RPxN	PxP
	see diagram	
11	RxP[3]	. . . .

WHITE TO PLAY

Black's two Bishops are more than compensated for by White's command of the Queen Rook file. Besides, Black has developed the wrong Bishop.

White wins material and maintains a winning attack

---

[1] Better is 8 . . . NxB; 9 RPxN, N–Q2; 10 R–Q1, P–KB3; 11 N–B3, B–N2 and Black is somewhat cramped, but his position remains defensible.

[2] This loses, as does 9 . . . PxP; 10 BxP†, KxB; 11 NxP† and 12 NxB. Black had to try 9 . . . BxN; 10 QxB, PxP and though Black has the worse of it, he should survive.

[3] If 11 . . . RxR; 12 QxP† and 13 QxR will cost Black a second Pawn.

Ruy Lopez

	WHITE	BLACK
1	P-K4	P-K4
2	N-KB3	N-QB3
3	B-N5	P-QR3
4	B-R4	N-B3
5	O-O	B-K2
6	R-K1	P-QN4
7	B-N3	O-O
8	P-B3	P-Q4[1]
9	PxP	NxP
10	NxP	NxN
11	RxN	N-B3[2]
12	P-Q4	B-Q3
13	R-K1[3]	N-N5
14	P-KR3	Q-R5
15	Q-B3	NxP
16	QxN?[4]	. . . .
	see diagram	
16	. . . .	B-R7†[5]
17	K-B1	B-N6[6]

Black has a winning attack

BLACK TO PLAY

Black sees the flaw in the obvious continuation, 16 . . . B–N6, but he has something dynamic in view.

---

[1] Introducing the famous Marshall Attack.

[2] 11 . . . P–QB3 also offers good attacking chances.

[3] 13 R–K2, anticipating a future attack on the King Bishop Pawn, is a good move here.

[4] The acceptance of the sacrifice loses. 16 R–K2 is quite playable.

[5] But not immediately 16 . . . B–N6 because of 17 QxP†!, RxQ; 18 R–K8 mate.

[6] Now if 18 QxP†? Black captures . . . RxQ with check and wins. Black's attack will now win by force, e.g. 18 Q–K2, BxP; 19 PxB, QR–K1; 20 QxR, QxP†; 21 K–K2 (or 21 K–N1, Q–R7†; 22 K–B1, Q–B7 mate), 21 . . . RxQ† and Black wins.

	WHITE	BLACK
1	P-K4	P-K4
2	N-KB3	N-QB3
3	B-N5	B-B4
4	P-B3	Q-B3[1]
5	P-Q4	PxP
6	P-K5	Q-N3[2]
7	PxP	NxQP[3]
8	NxN	Q-N3
	see diagram	
9	Q-N4!	N-K2[4]
10	P-K6!	P-QB3[5]
11	QxP	N-N3[6]
12	PxP†	K-Q1
13	N-K6†	PxN
14	B-N5†	. . . .[7]

WHITE TO PLAY

At first sight, it appears Black will regain the piece and remain a Pawn plus. But White is poised for a crushing attack.

White wins overwhelming material

---

[1] Not recommended, as the Queen is exposed too early. Preferable alternatives are 6 . . . KN–K2, 6 . . . N–B3, 6 . . . B–N3, or even the speculative 6 . . . P–B4.

[2] If 6 . . . NxP; 7 Q–K2, B–Q3; 8 PxP, White wins a piece.

[3] A faulty combination. Better chances are afforded by 7 . . . B–N5†; 8 N–B3, P–Q4, though the White game is still preferable.

[4] If 9 . . . BxN; 10 QxP and White will emerge the exchange ahead.

[5] If 10 . . . BxN; 11 PxQP†, K–Q1; 12 PxB=Q†, RxQ; 13 Q–Q7 mate, or 10 . . . PxP; 11 NxP!, QxB; 12 NxBP† or 10 . . . PxP; 11 NxP! BxP†; 12 K–Q1 remaining a piece ahead with an easy win.

[6] Or 11 . . . R–KB1; 12 B–KR6 or 11 . . . BxN; 12 PxP†, K–Q1; 13 P–B8=Q†.

[7] If 14 . . . K–B2 or 14 . . . K–Q2; 15 P–B8=Q† and if 14 . . . B–K2; 15 QxR†!, NxQ; 16 P–B8=Q†, etc.

	WHITE	BLACK
1	P-K4	P-K4
2	N-KB3	N-QB3
3	B-N5	P-QR3
4	B-R4	N-B3
5	O-O	NxP
6	P-Q4	P-QN4
7	B-N3	P-Q4
8	PxP	B-K3
9	P-B3	B-K2
10	R-K1	O-O
11	N-Q4	Q-Q2?[1]
	see diagram	
12	NxB	QxN[2]
13	RxN[3]	. . . .

White has won a Knight

WHITE TO PLAY

Black's last move has completed the development of all his pieces, while White's Queen Knight is still in the stable. Nevertheless, Black's Queen move was a fatal mistake.

---

[1] Black should play 11 . . . NxKP; 12 P–B3, B–Q3; 13 PxN, B–KN5 with a strong attack well worth the sacrificed piece. The text looks natural, but loses a piece for no compensation.

[2] Or 12 . . . PxN; 13 RxN and Black's Queen's Pawn is pinned on the file.

[3] Now the Queen Pawn is pinned on the diagonal and White has won a piece. This trap has claimed for its victims several well-known masters.

	WHITE	BLACK
1	P-K4	P-K4
2	N-KB3	N-QB3
3	B-N5	P-QR3
4	B-R4	N-B3
5	O-O	NxP
6	P-Q4	P-QN4
7	B-N3	P-Q4
8	PxP	B-K3
9	P-B3	B-QB4
10	Q-Q3	P-B3
11	PxP	QxP
12	BxP?[1]	O-O-O
13	BxB†	QxB
14	Q-K2[2]	KR-K1
15	B-K3[3]	. . . .

see diagram

15	. . . .	NxKBP
16	RxN	QxB
17	QxQ	R-Q8†[4]

**White will be checkmated
in three moves**

BLACK TO PLAY

White has played the opening carelessly, and he will pay dearly for the Pawn ahead, because all Black's forces are prepared to annihilate the enemy.

[1] This capture involves White in great difficulties. More discreet is 12 QN–Q2 with a good game for White.
[2] 14 Q-B2 is better, as White could then continue with 15 B-K3 which would give him some defensive chances.
[3] White is lost, for if 15 QN–Q2, NxKBP; 16 QxQ†, RxQ; and if 17 RxN, R–K7; 18 N–Q4, NxN!
[4] After 18 N–K1, RxN†; 19 R–B1, BxQ†; 20 K–R1, RxR is mate.

Ruy Lopez

	WHITE	BLACK
1	P-K4	P-K4
2	N-KB3	N-QB3
3	B-N5	P-QR3
4	B-R4	N-B3
5	O-O	NxP
6	P-Q4	P-QN4
7	B-N3	P-Q4
8	PxP	B-K3
9	P-B3	B-K2
10	B-K3	O-O
11	QN-Q2	P-B4[1]
12	PxP e.p.	NxP/3
13	N-N5	B-KB4[2]

see diagram

14	QN-K4	NxN
15	QxP†	K-R1[3]
16	Q-N8†	RxQ
17	N-B7	. . . .[4]

Black has been checkmated

WHITE TO PLAY

Black has completed his development, and there seem to be no weak spots in his position, but White is ready to unleash a winning attack.

[1] A better line is 11 . . . B–KN5; 12 NxN, PxN; 13 Q–Q5, QxQ; 14 BxQ, PxN; 15 BxN, PxP; 16 KxP, QR–Q1; 17 P–QR4, P–N5 and Black should draw without much difficulty.

[2] Or 13 . . . B–KN5; 14 P–B3 followed by 15 QN–K4! However, 13 . . . B–B2 is somewhat better than the text.

[3] This allows a forced mate but 15 . . . QxQ; 16 BxQ†, K–R1; 17 NxN gives White an extra Pawn in a superior position.

[4] The smothered mate scores again.

120

	WHITE	BLACK
1	P-K4	P-K4
2	N-KB3	N-QB3
3	B-N5	P-QR3
4	B-R4	N-B3
5	O-O	NxP
6	P-Q4	P-QN4
7	B-N3	P-Q4
8	P-QR4	P-N5[1]
9	P-R5	B-K2[2]
10	PxP	B-K3
	see diagram	
11	B-R4[3]	B-Q2[4]
12	QxP[5]	. . . .

White wins decisive material

WHITE TO PLAY

Black has developed too routinely. His last move was an irretrievable mistake. His Queen Bishop is needed on the Queen-side.

---

[1] Black should play 8 . . . NxQP with an excellent game.
[2] And now 9 . . . NxQP was absolutely necessary. The text loses.
[3] This pin wins a piece.
[4] Or 11 . . . Q–Q2; 12 N–Q4.
[5] White will win one of the two Knights.

Ruy Lopez

	WHITE	BLACK
1	P-K4	P-K4
2	N-KB3	N-QB3
3	B-N5	P-QR3
4	B-R4	N-B3
5	O-O	NxP
6	P-Q4	P-QN4
7	B-N3	P-Q4
8	NxP[1]	NxN
9	PxN	B-N2
10	B-K3	B-B4
11	Q-N4[2]	BxB!
12	QxP	....
	see diagram	
12	....	Q-N4!
13	QxR†[3]	K-K2
14	QxP	BxP†
15	K-R1[4]	R-KN1
16	Q-R3[5]	P-Q5
17	N-R3[6]	QxP†
18	QxQ	N-N6†
19	PxN	R-R1[7]

White has been checkmated

BLACK TO PLAY

White threatens to win the Exchange. Black, however, has a winning continuation, based on the masked power of his Queen Bishop.

---

[1] 8 PxP is the better move.
[2] 11 BxB is better. White overlooks Black's combination.
[3] If 13 QxQ, BxQ and Black is a piece ahead.
[4] If 15 RxB, Q-B8†; 16 R-B1, Q-K6†; 17 K-R1, N-B7†; 18 K-N1, N-R6†; 19 K-R1, Q-N8†; 20 RxQ, N-B7 mate.
[5] Or 16 P-N3, NxP†; 17 PxN, P-Q5†; 18 K-R2, QxP mate.
[6] Nothing else will do, either.
[7] A most attractive mate.

122

	WHITE	BLACK
1	P-K4	P-K4
2	N-KB3	N-QB3
3	B-N5	P-QR3
4	B-R4	N-B3
5	O-O	NxP
6	P-Q4	P-QN4
7	P-Q5	N-K2?[1]
8	R-K1	N-B4
9	NxP	PxB
	see diagram	
10	Q-B3	P-KB3
11	Q-R5†	P-N3
12	NxNP[2]	. . . .

WHITE TO PLAY

The Black King is in a strait-jacket, and only one convulsive gasp is permitted him.

Black will be checkmated or lose overwhelming material

---

[1] Black should play 7 . . . PxB; 8 PxN, P-Q3 with a good game.

[2] Naturally if 12 . . . PxN; 13 QxP mate. Black is unable to stave off mate.

	WHITE	BLACK
1	P-K4	P-K4
2	N-KB3	N-QB3
3	B-N5	N-Q5
4	NxN	PxN
5	B-B4[1]	N-B3
6	P-K5	P-Q4
7	B-N3	B-KN5
8	P-KB3[2]	N-K5!
9	O-O[3]	P-Q6
10	PxB	....

see diagram

10	....	B-B4†
11	K-R1	N-N6†
12	PxN	Q-N4
13	R-B5[4]	P-KR4
14	PxRP[5]	QxR
15	P-N4[6]	RxP†
16	PxR	Q-K5
17	Q-B3[7]	Q-R5†
18	Q-R3	Q-K8†
19	K-R2	B-N8†
20	K-R1	B-B7†
21	K-R2	Q-N8

White has been checkmated

BLACK TO PLAY

White has nothing better than to capture the Bishop, which appears to have slowed down Black's attack. But Black's elegant offer of another piece forces checkmate.

---

[1] Preferable at this point is 5 O-O.
[2] It looks as though White is winning a piece.
[3] Not 9 PxB, Q-R5†; 10 K-K2 (10 P-N3, NxNP also wins for Black) 10 ... Q-B7†; 11 K-Q3, N-B4 mate.
[4] Black threatened 13 ... Q-R3 mate.
[5] Now if 14 RxQ, PxP†; 15 R-R5, RxR mate.
[6] Black again threatened 15 ... QxP† or 15 ... RxP† with mate.
[7] The only defense against 17 ... Q-R5 mate.

124

	WHITE	BLACK
1	P-K4	P-K4
2	N-KB3	N-QB3
3	B-N5	N-Q5
4	B-B4[1]	B-B4
5	NxP?[2]	....
	see diagram	
5	....	Q-N4[3]
6	NxBP[4]	QxP
7	R-B1[5]	QxKP†
8	B-K2	N-B6

White has been checkmated

BLACK TO PLAY ....

White has grabbed a Pawn and threatens Black's vulnerable King Bishop. Black disregards the threat with fatal consequences to the White forces.

---

[1] Weak. White should play 4 NxN, PxN; 5 O-O.

[2] Either 5 NxN or 5 O-O would give White a good game. The text loses.

[3] This clever move, which attacks the Knight and King Knight Pawn, wins.

[4] Or 6 P-KB4, QxNP; 7 R-B1, QxKP†; 8 K-B2, N-B4† or 6 N-N4, P-Q4! attacking the Bishop and uncovering on the Knight. Probably White's best chance was 6 BxP†, K-K2; 7 O-O, although he would have to play with a piece down.

[5] If 7 NxR, QxP†; 8 B-B1, QxP†; 9 B-K2, NxP†; 10 K-B1, Q-R8 mate.

Scotch Gambit

	WHITE	BLACK
1	P-K4	P-K4
2	N-KB3	N-QB3
3	P-Q4	PxP
4	NxP	KN-K2[1]
5	N-QB3	P-KN3?[2]
6	B-KN5!	B-N2[3]
	see diagram	
7	N-Q5[4]	....

**White wins decisive
material, or Black
is checkmated**

WHITE TO PLAY

In this innocent looking position, White wins by force. The continuation includes a variation wherein White sacrifices his Queen.

---

[1] This is inferior. Either 4 ... N–B3 or 4 ... B–B4 are recommended, leading to easy equality.

[2] And this move, severely weakening the Black squares on the King-side, is definitely bad. Preferable was 5 ... NxN; 6 QxN, N–B3 with a playable game.

[3] There is no effective answer to the threat of 7 N–Q5, e.g. 6 ... P–KR3; 7 N–Q5, PxB; 8 N–B6 mate.

[4] Winning. The main point is that 7 ... BxN can be met by 8 QxB, and if 8 ... NxQ; 9 N–B6†, K–B1; 10 B–R6 mate.

126

Scotch Gambit

	WHITE	BLACK
1	P-K4	P-K4
2	N-KB3	N-QB3
3	P-Q4	PxP
4	NxP	NxN?[1]
5	QxN	P-Q3
6	N-B3	N-B3
7	B-KB4	B-K3
8	O-O-O	B-K2
9	P-K5	PxP
10	QxKP	B-Q3
11	B-N5†	N-Q2[2]
	see diagram	
12	RxB	PxR
13	QxNP	R-KB1[3]
14	BxP	....[4]

White wins overwhelming material

WHITE TO PLAY

Here, the obvious 12 QxP fails because of 12 ... BxB†. So White gets rid of the Bishop by giving up a Rook for it. This leaves Black without resource.

---

[1] This exchange merely facilitates White's development. Either 4 ... N-B3 or 4 ... B-B4 is good.
[2] This loses by force. Black had to play 11 ... K-B1.
[3] If 13 ... K-K2; 14 B-N5† wins.
[4] Black has no effective defense against 15 QxR mate.

Sicilian Defense

	WHITE	BLACK
1	P-K4	P-QB4
2	N-KB3	N-QB3
3	P-Q4	PxP
4	NxP	P-KN3
5	N-QB3	B-N2
6	B-K3	N-B3
7	B-QB4	P-QR3
8	O-O	P-Q3
9	K-R1	B-Q2
10	B-N3	P-QN4
11	P-QR3	R-QB1
	see diagram	
12	N-Q5!	NxP?[1]
13	NxNP!	N-B4[2]
14	BxN	PxB
15	NxP![3]	....

White will gain decisive material

WHITE TO PLAY

By abandoning material, White conceives an elegant maneuver which wins in all variations.

[1] Black nibbles at the hook. 12 ... O-O or 12 ... KNxN was playable.

[2] If 13 ... PxN; 14 B-N6, R-B2; 15 NxR†, K-B1; 16 N-K6† wins the Queen.

[3] Very pretty. The Knight at K7 cannot be captured without material loss for Black, e.g. 15 ... QxN; 16 R-K1, B-K3 (if Black interposes at K4, then 17 N-Q6†, 18 NxR and 19 P-KB4 and White has won the exchange in a highly favorable position); 17 N-Q6† and wins: if 17 ... K-B1; 18 NxR and if 17 ... K-Q1; 18 NxBP†, K-B2; 19 RxB!, QxN (other Queen moves can be met by 20 NxR); 20 RxN† wins the Queen.
If 15 ... NxN; 16 N-Q6†, K-B1; 17 NxP, Q-B2; 18 NxR, BxN; 19 Q-B3†, N-B4 (not 19 ... B-B4; 20 P-N4. Now if 20 P-N4?, B-QB3 breaks the pin); 20 Q-Q5 with Rook and two Pawns and a strong attack against the vulnerable King for the two pieces, e.g. 20 ... P-B5; 21 BxP or 20 ... N-R3; 21 QR-Q1.
Finally, if 15 ... KxN; 16 Q-Q6†, K-K1; 17 KR-K1†, B-K3 (if Black interposes at K4 with Knight or Bishop, White plays RxN† [or Bishop] and wins the King Rook with check); 18 RxB† and wins, for if 18 ... PxR; 19 QxP†, N-K2; 20 N-Q6† or 18 ... N-K2; 19 QR-K1.
Probably best is 15 ... PxN; 16 NxR, BxN, but then White has 17 Q-K2† followed by 18 QxNP and White has somewhat the better chances.

128

	WHITE	BLACK
1	P-K4	P-QB4
2	N-KB3	P-Q3
3	P-Q4	PxP
4	NxP	N-KB3
5	N-QB3	P-KN3
6	P-B4	B-N2?[1]

see diagram

7	P-K5	PxP
8	PxP	N-Q4[2]
9	B-N5†	K-B1
10	O-O	BxP?[3]
11	B-R6†	K-N1[4]
12	NxN	QxN
13	N-B5[5]	Q-B4†
14	B-K3	Q-B2[6]
15	N-R6†	K-B1[7]
16	RxP mate	

Black has been checkmated

WHITE TO PLAY

Black has developed "normally" and seems prepared to castle safely. Black's last move, however, was a mistake.

---

[1] This normal-looking move is a mistake. Black should play 6 . . . N–B3; 7 NxN, PxN; 8 P–K5, N–Q2 with equal chances.

[2] If 8 . . . KN–Q2; 9 P–K6 is strong and 8 . . . N–N5 loses a piece to 9 B–N5†, e.g. if 9 . . . B–Q2 or 9 . . . N–Q2; 10 QxN, while 9 . . . K–B1; 10 N–K6† wins Black's Queen.

[3] This is an error, but good moves are at a premium. 10 . . . NxN loses immediately to 11 N–K6†. Perhaps 10 . . . K–N1 is comparatively best.

[4] Forced, for if 11 . . . B–N2; 12 BxB†, KxB; 13 NxN wins a piece for 13 . . . QxN; 14 N–B5† costs the Queen.

[5] And White threatens 14 NxP mate, as well as 14 QxQ.

[6] The threat was 15 Q–Q8 mate.

[7] 15 . . . K–N2 meets with the same mate.

Sicilian Defense

	WHITE	BLACK
1	P-K4	P-QB4
2	N-KB3	N-QB3
3	P-Q4	PxP
4	NxP	P-KN3
5	N-QB3	B-N2
6	B-K3	N-B3
7	B-QB4	O-O
8	B-N3	N-QR4?[1]
9	P-K5	N-K1?[2]
	see diagram	
10	BxP†[3]	....

White wins the Queen for two pieces, or Black is checkmated

WHITE TO PLAY

Though the Black Knights are awkwardly placed, Black has apparently castled into safety. What has he to fear? White quickly answers the question.

[1] Black should play either 8 ... N-KN5! or 8 ... P-Q3. The text loses at least two active minor pieces for a Rook and Pawns.

[2] This costs the Queen. Comparatively best was 9 ... NxB; 10 KPxN!, NxR; 11 PxB, NxP†; 12 QxN, KxP, though White has a winning advantage. If 9 ... N-KR4, simply 10 P-KN4 wins a piece for White.

[3] And White wins the Queen or mates, e.g. 10 ... KxB (if 10 ... RxB; 11 N-K6! and the Queen is trapped) 11 N-K6, KxN (again the Queen has no safe move); 12 Q-Q5†, K-B4 and with the Black King so vulnerable, White has several attractive methods of winning, perhaps the simplest being 13 P-K6†, B-K4 (if 13 ... K-B3; 14 B-N5 mate, and 13 ... K-N5; 14 Q-N5 mates); 14 P-KB4, followed in most variations by 15 PxN and 16 R-B1† with a quick mate.

130

Sicilian Defense

BLACK TO PLAY

White is unaware that his last move has enormously increased the power of Black's Queen. Black starts his combination by sacrificing the Exchange.

	WHITE	BLACK
1	P-K4	P-QB4
2	N-KB3	N-QB3
3	P-Q4	PxP
4	NxP	N-B3
5	N-QB3	P-Q3
6	B-K2	P-KN3
7	O-O	B-N2
8	B-K3	O-O
9	N-N3	P-QR3
10	P-QR4	B-K3
11	N-Q4	NxN
12	BxN	Q-R4
13	P-B4	QR-B1
14	B-B3	R-B5
15	R-K1[1]	N-N5
16	N-K2?[2]	....
	see diagram	
16	....	RxB
17	NxR	QxR†
18	QxQ	BxN†
19	K-R1[3]	N-B7†[4]

Black wins overwhelming material

---

[1] 15 K–R1 holds the balance, for 15 . . . NxP?; 16 BxB wins, and 15 . . . Q–N5 can be met by 16 N–R2, Q–R4 (16 . . . QxP; 17 P–N3 or 16 . . . RxB; 17 NxQ) ; 17 N–B3.

[2] This allows a beautiful combination, but White's position was already quite bad (16 BxB, Q–B4†). Relatively best was 16 P–K5.

[3] If 19 K–B1, B–B5†; 20 B–K2, NxP mate.

[4] Black will be a piece ahead after 20 K–N1, N–Q6†.

Sicilian Defense

	WHITE	BLACK
1	P-K4	P-QB4
2	N-KB3	N-QB3
3	P-Q4	PxP
4	NxP	N-B3
5	N-QB3	P-Q3
6	B-KN5	P-K3
7	Q-Q2	B-K2
8	O-O-O	O-O
9	N/4-N5[1]	Q-R4
10	BxN	BxB
11	QxP?[2]	. . . .

see diagram

11	. . . .	P-QR3
12	N-R3[3]	B-N4†
13	K-N1[4]	R-Q1
14	Q-N3	RxR†
15	NxR	Q-Q7![5]

White cannot avoid checkmate

BLACK TO PLAY

White has captured the White Queen Pawn, but as a result Black captures the Queen File with deadly effect.

---

[1] 9 P–B4 was better. White is off in search of a tainted Pawn.

[2] Consistently wrong. Actually, 11 NxQP offered better chances for equality.

[3] Forced; if 12 N–B7, B–K4 wins the Knight.

[4] If 13 P–B4, R–Q1 traps the Queen.

[5] There is no effective defense to the threats of 16 . . . Q–B8 mate, and 16 . . . QxN mate, for if 16 N–K3, Q–K8† and mate next.

132

Sicilian Defense

	WHITE	BLACK
1	P-K4	P-QB4
2	N-KB3	P-K3
3	P-Q4	PxP
4	NxP	N-KB3
5	N-QB3	B-N5[1]
6	P-K5	N-Q4
7	Q-N4	P-KN3
8	P-QR3	Q-R4?[2]
	see diagram	
9	PxB	QxR
10	N-N3[3]	. . . .

WHITE TO PLAY

Black sees no reason why he should not develop another piece while retaining all threats. But he has overlooked the main theme.

Black's Queen is trapped

---

[1] Not a good move, as it ceded the initiative to White.

[2] Thinking to win material by the threefold attack on the White pinned Knight, and the Rook Pawn is pinned by the Queen. Better was 8 . . . BxN†.

[3] Once again the trapper is trapped. Black's Queen is embarrassed for a move.

Sicilian Defense

	WHITE	BLACK
1	P-K4	P-QB4
2	N-KB3	N-QB3
3	P-Q4	PxP
4	NxP	N-B3
5	N-QB3	P-Q3
6	B-KN5	P-K3
7	NxN	PxN
8	P-K5	Q-R4[1]
	see diagram	
9	B-N5![2]	PxB
10	PxN	P-N5
11	Q-B3!?	PxN[3]
12	Q-B6†[4]	. . . .

Black is hopelessly lost

WHITE TO PLAY

Black's last move seems to hold his central Pawn formation, but he overlooks White's startling maneuver, a combination of interposition and sacrifice.

---

[1] A simpler line for Black is 8 . . . PxP; 9 Q-B3, B-K2; 10 BxN (or 10 QxP†, B-Q2; 11 Q-B3, P-K5; 12 NxP, NxN!; 13 BxB, Q-R4†! with advantage to Black). 10 . . . BxB; 11 QxP†, B-Q2; 12 Q-B3, O-O; 13 B-Q3, R-N1 and Black stands well.

[2] 9 BxN, PxB; 10 PxP, Q-K4† leads to equality. The text is speculative.

[3] 11 . . . Q-K4† gives Black the advantage.

[4] The check must be respected.

134

Sicilian Defense

	WHITE	BLACK
1	P-K4	P-QB4
2	N-KB3	N-QB3
3	P-Q4	PxP
4	NxP	N-B3
5	N-QB3	P-Q3
6	B-KN5[1]	P-K3
7	NxN[2]	PxN
8	P-K5	Q-R4
9	BxN	PxB
10	PxQP	Q-K4†
11	B-K2[3]	BxP
12	Q-Q3	QR-N1
13	O-O-O	K-K2
14	P-KN3	R-Q1
15	Q-K4[4]	....

see diagram

| 15 | .... | QxN[5] |

Black wins decisive material

BLACK TO PLAY

White is poised to swap Queens, in which case he will have a better endgame because of his superior Pawn formation. Black, however, instead of giving Queen for Queen, offers Queen for Knight!

---

[1] This is the famous Richter Attack, designed to prevent White from continuing with 6 ... P-KN3 (Dragon Variation).

[2] This and White's next move are tricky, but confer no advantage to White. Better is 7 Q-Q2, with P-KB4 soon to follow.

[3] 11 Q-K2 is safer and better. With Queens on the board, Black obtains a dangerous initiative.

[4] This loses immediately, although the White game was already very difficult.

[5] After 16 PxQ, B-R6 is mate. White is lost.

Sicilian Defense

	WHITE	BLACK
1	P-K4	P-QB4
2	N-KB3	P-Q3
3	P-Q4	PxP
4	NxP	N-KB3
5	N-QB3	P-QR3
6	B-QB4	P-K3
7	B-N3	P-QN4
8	P-B4	B-N2
9	O-O	P-N5
10	P-K5	PxN
11	PxN	N-Q2?[1]

see diagram

12	P-B5!	P-K4
13	BxP†![2]	KxB
14	Q-R5†	K-N1[3]
15	P-B7	. . . .

Black has been checkmated

WHITE TO PLAY

Black now threatens to capture White's forward King Bishop Pawn; it is that very Pawn, however, that will destroy the Black King.

---

[1] 11 . . . QxP was better, though White will still enjoy a fine attack after 12 P–B5!

[2] The knockout blow.

[3] The quick way out. Black could resist longer with 14 . . . P–N3; 15 PxP†, PxP; 16 QxR, PxN; 17 Q–R7†, K–K3; 18 Q–N8†, K–K4; 19 B–B4†, KxP; 20 QR–K1 he will be mated in a few more moves.

136

Sicilian Defense

	WHITE	BLACK
1	P-K4	P-QB4
2	N-KB3	P-Q3
3	P-Q4	PxP
4	NxP	N-KB3
5	N-QB3	P-QR3
6	B-KN5	QN-Q2
7	B-QB4	P-K3?[1]
8	O-O	Q-B2?[2]
	see diagram	
9	BxKP	PxB
10	NxP	Q-B5
11	N-Q5![3]	. . . .

WHITE TO PLAY

Black, attacking a Bishop, is unaware of the weaknesses in his central Pawn front. The attacked Bishop strikes first!

White has a winning attack

---

[1] 7 . . . Q–B2 is the proper move, and if 8 B–N3, P–K3; 9 O–O, N–B4 and Black has fair chances.

[2] Now this move is a blunder, as it allows a winning sacrifice.

[3] With his two Pawns and tremendous attack for the gambited piece, White must win. Neither the Black King nor Queen is safe. White is now threatening (after 11 . . . NxN; 12 PxN), 13 P–QN3, driving the Queen away from Black's QB2.

Sicilian Defense

	WHITE	BLACK
1	P-K4	P-QB4
2	N-KB3	P-Q3
3	P-Q4	PxP
4	NxP	N-KB3
5	N-QB3	P-QR3
6	P-KR3	P-QN4?[1]
7	N-Q5!	B-N2[2]
8	NxN†	NPxN
9	P-QB4	PxP?[3]
10	BxP	BxP?[4]

see diagram

11	O-O	P-Q4
12	R-K1!	P-K4?[5]
13	Q-R4†	N-Q2[6]
14	RxB!	PxR
15	N-B5[7]	....

White will mount a forceful attack

WHITE TO PLAY

Black's Bishop at K5 seems dominantly placed in view of ...P-Q4. But White is ready to show up the weaknesses in Black's game.

---

[1] 6 ... N-B3 is preferable.

[2] 7 ... P-K3, avoiding doubled Pawns, is better, but not 7 ... NxP; 8 Q-B3, N-B4; 9 N-B6†, KPxN; 10 QxR, B-N2; 11 Q-R7, P-K4; 12 P-QN4 and White wins.

[3] 9 ... BxP; 10 PxP, B-KN2; 11 Q-N4, B-N3; 12 N-B5 is bad, but Black could try 9 ... P-N5; 10 B-Q3, Q-Q2.

[4] Black is definitely too avaricious. 10 ... Q-R4†; 11 B-Q2, Q-K4 poses thornier problems to White.

[5] White's attack is promising no matter how Black plays, but 12 ... P-K3, so as not to relinquish control of his KB4 square, is a sterner defense.

[6] 13 ... Q-Q2 loses to 14 B-QN5.

[7] Surprisingly, Black is quite helpless, e.g. 15 ... R-KN1; 16 BxP†, KxB; 17 Q-N3†, K-N3 (17 ... K-K1; 18 Q-K6†, B-K2; 19 N-Q6†, K-B1; 20 Q-B7 mate); 18 QxR†, KxN; 19 P-N4 mate, or 15 ... B-B4; 16 N-N7†, K-K2; 17 N-B5†, K-K1; 18 B-K3, BxB; 19 PxB, Q-N3 (the threat was 20 Q-N4); 20 BxP†, KxB; 21 QxN†, K-N3; 22 Q-N7†, KxN; 23 Q-N4 mate, or here 20 ... K-Q1; 21 R-Q1, Q-N4; 22 Q-R3 and White wins quickly as he threatens 23 Q-K7† followed by either 24 R-B1† or 24 N-Q6† depending on Black's moves.

138

	WHITE	BLACK
1	P-K4	P-QB4
2	N-KB3	P-Q3
3	P-Q4	PxP
4	NxP	N-KB3
5	N-QB3	P-QR3
6	B-KN5	QN-Q2
7	B-QB4	P-K3
8	O-O	Q-R4
9	Q-Q2	P-N4?[1]

see diagram

10	B-Q5![2]	PxB
11	PxP	B-N2
12	QR-K1†	K-Q1
13	N-B6†	BxN
14	PxB	N-B4[3]
15	Q-Q4[4]	. . . .

White has a winning attack

WHITE TO PLAY

White's attacked Bishop will initiate a maneuver undermining the Black position. The coup is based on the insecurity of the Black Queen Rook and the Black King.

[1] Premature. 9 . . . B-K2 is preferable.

[2] This wins as in the previous example. The Black King in the center of the board is a sitting duck.

[3] Other Knight moves are no better, e.g. 14 . . . N-K4; 15 RxN, or 14 . . . N-N3; 15 Q-Q4, K-B2; 16 BxN, PxB; 17 QxP, and if 14 . . . N-N1; 15 BxN, PxB; 16 Q-K3, K-B2; 17 P-QN4, Q-R6; 17 QxN†, PxB; 16 Q-K3, K-B2; 17 P-QN4, followed by 18 N-Q5† wins the Queen.

[4] Now Black can only try 15 . . . N-K3; 16 BxN†, K-B1; 17 RxN, PxR; 18 BxP, R-KN1; 19 BxB, RxB; 20 Q-N7 winning easily.

Sicilian Defense

	WHITE	BLACK
1	P-K4	P-QB4
2	N-KB3	P-Q3
3	P-Q4	PxP
4	QxP	N-QB3
5	B-QN5	B-Q2
6	BxN	BxB[1]
7	N-B3	P-K3
8	B-N5	N-B3
9	0-0-0	B-K2
10	P-K5	PxP
11	QxKP	Q-N1
12	Q-K2	0-0
13	N-K5	Q-B2[2]
14	R-Q3	N-Q4
15	B-Q2	QR-B1
16	R-R3	NxN[3]
17	BxN	BxP??[4]

see diagram

| 18 | R-N3 | BxR |
| 19 | RxP†![5] | |

White has an overwhelming attack

WHITE TO PLAY

White knows that the best defense against attack (his Bishop is menaced) is counter-attack. White will open lines against an insecure King.

---

[1] This is not bad, but the recapture with the Pawn affords more opportunity for active counterplay in the center.

[2] 13 . . . BxP?; 14 KR-N1 gives White too strong an attack on the open file.

[3] White has built up a dangerous attack, and Black needs a constructive plan for the defense. 16 . . . P-KN3, hoping to get in 17 . . . B-B3 was indicated.

[4] And this loses by force. 17 . . . P-B3; 18 Q-R5!, B-K5! (not 18 . . . PxN; 19 BxP, followed by 20 QxP† and wins) and Black still has chances of holding, though White has the edge with 19 P-B3.

[5] If 19 . . . KxR; 20 Q-N4†, K-B3 (20 . . . K-R1; 21 NxP mates and 20 . . . K-R3; 21 B-Q2†, B-N4; 22 QxB mate); 21 N-Q7 mate, and if 19 . . . K-R1; 20 R-N8†!, RxR (20 . . . KxR; 21 Q-N4†, K-R1; 22 NxP mate); 21 NxP or 21 N-N6 mate.

140

Sicilian Defense

WHITE TO PLAY

Black has advanced his Queen-side Pawns, and White now takes dazzling advantage of this weakening of the KR1–QR8 diagonal.

	WHITE	BLACK
1	P-K4	P-QB4
2	N-KB3	P-Q3
3	P-Q4	PxP
4	NxP	N-KB3
5	N-QB3	P-QR3
6	B-N5	QN-Q2
7	B-QB4	P-K3
8	O-O	P-R3
9	B-R4	Q-R4
10	Q-Q2	P-QN4?[1]
	see diagram	
11	B-Q5![2]	PxB
12	PxP	P-N4
13	QR-K1†	N-K4
14	P-B4	N-Q2
15	PxN	PxP[3]
16	B-N3	P-B3
17	K-R1[4]	....

White has regained his material and maintains a strong attack

---

[1] Premature. 10 . . . B–K2 or 10 . . . N–K4 is preferable.

[2] Black's King in the center of the board is the target. The Bishop must be captured, or 12 N–B6 wins the exchange.

[3] Naturally not 15 . . . PxB; 16 PxP†, K–Q1; 17 N–B6 mate.

[4] Black's many weaknesses and his exposed King will make a successful defense impossible.

Sicilian Defense

	WHITE	BLACK
1	P-K4	P-QB4
2	N-KB3	P-Q3
3	P-Q4	PxP
4	NxP	N-KB3
5	N-QB3	P-QR3
6	B-N5	QN-Q2
7	B-K2	P-K3
8	O-O	Q-B2
9	B-R5	Q-B5?

see diagram

10	NxP!²	QxN
11	N-Q5	K-Q1
12	B-N4³	. . . .

White wins overwhelming material

WHITE TO PLAY

Black's last move is meant to stop White's NxP. But White makes the move, anyway.

¹ The correct method of defending against the threat of 10 NxP was 9 ... NxB; 10 QxN; N-B3 with fair prospects.

² An attractive combination which succeeds because of the constricted nature of Black's development and the awkward development of the Black King and Queen.

³ White should recapture the sacrificed piece and remain with an extra Pawn or a winning attack, e.g. 12 ... Q-K1; 13 Q-Q2! (other possibilities here such as 13 BxN, BxB; 14 Q-Q4, K-B1 or 14 NxN, PxN; 15 BxP†, B-K2; 16 QxP or 16 BxR are promising but not completely convincing), 13 ... P-QR4 (Black must guard against the threat of 14 BxN and 15 Q-R5†); 14 BxN, BxB; 15 Q-B3, Q-K4; 16 QxQ, PxQ; 17 NxN and White has extra material which should win. In this variation, too, White has other tempting tries, but Black seems to have adequate defensive resources at his disposal.

142

Sicilian Defense

	WHITE	BLACK
1	P-K4	P-QB4
2	N-KB3	P-Q3
3	P-Q4	PxP
4	NxP	N-KB3
5	N-QB3	P-QR3
6	B-KN5	QN-Q2
7	Q-B3	P-QN4?[1]
	see diagram	
8	P-K5!	PxP
9	QxR	PxN
10	N-Q5	N-K5?[2]
11	Q-B6[3]	

WHITE TO PLAY

Black over-rated his counter-chances after the obvious loss of the Exchange.

White wins overwhelming material

---

[1] 7 ... P-K3 is better. The text move sacrifices the exchange unsoundly.

[2] Precipitates the end. Though he should certainly lose, Black could fight on with 10 ... NxN; 11 QxN, P-B3 and 12 ... P-K4.

[3] The finisher; White wins at least another piece, e.g. 11 ... P-KB3 (otherwise Black loses his Queen after 12 N-B7†); 12 N-B7†, K-B2; 13 Q-K6†, K-N3; 14 QxN† and if 14 ... KxB; 15 N-K6†.

Sicilian Defense

	WHITE	BLACK
1	P-K4	P-QB4
2	N-KB3	P-Q3
3	P-Q4	PxP
4	NxP	N-KB3
5	N-QB3	P-QR3
6	P-KN3	P-QN4[1]
7	B-N2	B-N2
8	O-O	QN-Q2
9	R-K1	P-K3?[2]

see diagram

10	P-K5!	BxB
11	PxN	B-N2
12	PxP	BxP
13	N-B5![3]	. . . .

White has many winning continuations

WHITE TO PLAY

Black's development seemingly has followed theoretical routine. But White shows the inadequacy of routine "routine".

---

[1] 6 . . . P-K4 leads to a better setup, offering good opportunities for counterplay.

[2] Overlooking White's reply. It was important to defend his Queen Bishop with 9 . . . Q-B2. White still has the advantage with 10 P-QR4, and if 10 . . . P-N5; 11 N-Q5—but it's still a game.

[3] Winning at least a Pawn. Black's best is probably 13 . . . O-O yielding the Queen Pawn, but not 13 . . . B-KB1; 14 RxP†!, PxR; 15 Q-R5 mate.

144   *Sicilian Defense*

WHITE TO PLAY

Black threatens 18 . . . B–K3, hoping to simplify with a playable game. Nevertheless, White does permit Black's Bishop sortie, which, however, cannot avert disaster.

	WHITE	BLACK
1	P-K4	P-QB4
2	N-KB3	P-Q3
3	P-Q4	PxP
4	NxP	N-KB3
5	N-QB3	P-QR3
6	B-K2	P-K4
7	N-N3	B-K2
8	B-K3	QN-Q2[1]
9	P-N4[2]	P-R3
10	P-KR4	P-QN4
11	P-QR4	P-N5
12	N-Q5	NxN
13	QxN	R-QN1
14	B-QB4	O-O[3]
15	P-N5	PxP
16	PxP	N-N3[4]
17	BxN	QxB
	see diagram	
18	P-N6	B-K3
19	QxB[5]	. . . .

White mates in a few moves

---

[1] 8 . . . B–K3 is better here; then 9 P–N4 could be met strongly by 9 . . . P–Q4.

[2] An interesting idea whereby White strives for P–N5 in order to achieve a King-side attack and obtain control of the vital Q5 square.

[3] This is too risky; the King is much safer in the center and so 14 . . . R–KB1 is to be preferred.

[4] White has a tremendous attack no matter how Black plays, e.g. 16 . . . B–N2; 17 Q–Q1, P–N3; 18 Q–N4, N–N3; 19 BxN, QxB; 20 O–O–O, K–N2; 21 R–R7†, KxR; 22 Q–R4†, K–N1 (or 22 . . . K–N2; 23 Q–R6†, K–N1; 24 R–R1); 23 R–R1, BxP†; 24 QxB, P–Q4; 25 Q–R6 and wins.

[5] 19 . . . PxQ; 20 BxP†, R–B2; 21 BxR† (or 21 . . . PxR†), K–B1; 22 R–R8 mate.

Sicilian Defense

	WHITE	BLACK
1	P-K4	P-QB4
2	N-KB3	P-Q3
3	P-Q4	PxP
4	NxP	N-KB3
5	N-QB3	P-K3
6	P-B4	B-K2
7	B-Q3	O-O
8	O-O	P-QR3
9	K-R1	Q-B2
10	Q-K2	N-B3
11	NxN	PxN
12	P-K5	N-Q4
13	PxP	BxP
14	B-Q2	P-QR4[1]
15	N-K4	NxP[2]

WHITE TO PLAY

Of course, White must get rid of the Knight, but there is a better way to capture it than the most obvious.

see diagram

	WHITE	BLACK
16	RxN	BxR
17	N-B6†	PxN[3]
18	Q-N4†	B-N4[4]
19	BxB	PxB
20	QxP†	K-R1
21	Q-R6	. . . .

White mates next move

---

[1] The Pawn is tainted, e.g. 14 . . . BxP; 15 NxN, and 14 . . . NxP; 15 BxN, BxB; 16 Q-K4.

[2] Black should play 15 . . . B-K2. The capture is still too risky.

[3] If 17 . . . K-R1; 18 Q-K4, P-N3; 19 BxB wins easily.

[4] Or 18 . . . K-R1; 19 BxB, Q-Q1 (not 19 . . . P-K4; 20 Q-R4, P-B4; 21 Q-B6†, K-N1; 22 B-R6).

146

	WHITE	BLACK
1	P-K4	P-QB4
2	P-QB3	N-QB3[1]
3	P-Q4	PxP
4	PxP	P-Q4
5	N-QB3	PxP?[2]
6	P-Q5	N-K4
7	Q-R4†!	B-Q2[3]
8	QxKP	N-N3
	see diagram	
9	N-N5!	N-B3?[4]
10	N-Q6	. . . .

Black is checkmated

WHITE TO PLAY

White has already moved his Queen twice in the opening flurry, and now Black is prepared to attack the Queen with gain of another tempo. White has an astounding rebuttal.

[1] An immediate 2 . . . P–Q4 is simpler.

[2] 5 . . . P–K3 or 5 . . . N–B3 are safer and preferable.

[3] 7 . . . Q–Q2 loses to 8 B–QN5, and 7 . . . N–Q2 is met by 8 B–KB4 with 9 N–N5 in the offing.

[4] Black's game is very bad since he cannot play 9 . . . BxN (10 BxB† wins the Queen) and 9 . . . Q–N3 is met by 10 B–K3 and White still has the annoying threats on Q6 and QB7. Probably best is 9 . . . B–B1 when 10 P–Q6 should win. The text is a radical method of dealing with his problems.

Sicilian Defense

WHITE	BLACK
1 P-K4	P-QB4
2 P-QB3	P-Q4
3 P-K5[1]	B-B4
4 P-Q4	PxP[2]
5 PxP	BxN?[3]
6 RxB	Q-R4†
7 B-Q2	QxP??
see diagram	
8 B-B3[4]	. . . .

**Black's Queen will be
trapped**

WHITE TO PLAY

*Black has exercised his most
important piece to pick off
White's isolated weakling
Pawn. Too much force has
been exhausted for a puny reward. White is prepared to
punish Black's folly.*

[1] More in the spirit of the opening is 3 PxP, QxP; 4 P–Q4. Black has
an easy game after the text.

[2] 4 . . . P–K3 gives Black a very comfortable game.

[3] The beginning of an unfortunate plan to win a Pawn. 5 . . . P–K3
was still good.

[4] 9 R–R1 will trap the Black Queen.

148   *Sicilian Defense*

	WHITE	BLACK
1	P-K4	P-QB4
2	N-KB3	N-KB3
3	P-K5	N-Q4
4	P-QN3	P-KN3
5	B-N2	B-N2
6	P-B4	N-B2
7	N-B3	P-Q3?[1]
8	PxP	PxP
9	P-Q4	PxP
10	NxP	O-O
11	B-K2	P-Q4
12	PxP	NxP
13	NxN	QxN
14	O-O	R-Q1[2]
15	B-B4!	Q-K5
16	R-K1	Q-B5[3]
17	R-K7	BxN[4]
	see diagram	
18	RxBP!	BxP†
19	K-R1	RxQ†
20	RxR[5]	. . . .

WHITE TO PLAY

Black threatens to win White's Queen. White is agreeable to the deal, because in exchange for the lady he'll capture the Black King.

Black cannot avoid mate

---

[1] This strategy is inconsistent. Black has a fine game with 7 . . . N–B3, and if 8 N–K4, N–K3, laying siege to the White King Pawn.

[2] Somewhat better was 14 . . . N–B3, but Black's backward development still makes his game awkward.

[3] Not 16 . . . RxN; 17 BxR, QxB; 18 R–K8†, winning the Queen.

[4] On 17 . . . B–K3; 18 NxB!, RxQ†; 19 RxR and Black is defenseless against the various threats such as 20 R–Q8† and 20 NxQ, for if 19 . . . PxN; 20 RxB† and 21 R–Q8† mates.

[5] If 20 . . . QxR; 21 R–Q8 mates, and 20 . . . QxB; 21 R–N7† and 22 R–Q8† mates.

	WHITE	BLACK
1	P-K4	P-QB4
2	N-K2	N-QB3
3	P-Q4	PxP
4	NxP	P-K4
5	N-N5	P-Q3
6	N/1-B3	P-QR3
7	N-R3	P-B4[1]
8	N-B4	PxP?
9	NxP/4	P-Q4
	see diagram	
10	B-N5[2]	KN-K2
11	N/K-Q6†	K-Q2
12	N-B7	Q-K1[3]
13	N/4-Q6[4]	. . . .

Black loses his Queen

WHITE TO PLAY

A seemingly disastrous Pawn fork against White's two Knights will be refuted by an irrefutable attack against the Black Queen.

---

[1] This premature opening of the game when Black is behind in development is too risky. Better is 7 . . . P–QN4 to prevent the Knight at R3 from entering the game for awhile.

[2] Black has overlooked or underestimated the effectiveness of this move. If now 10 . . . B–K2; 11 N(K)–Q6†, K–Q2 (or 11 . . . K–B1; 12 QxP! and the threat of Q–B7 mate is decisive); 12 N–B7 and White, who eyes the Queen Pawn and 13 N–N6† as well as NxR wins quite easily.

[3] If 12 . . . Q–B2; 13 NxR, winning a Rook, is simplest, though other moves also win.

150

	WHITE	BLACK
1	P-K4	P-QB4
2	N-KB3	N-QB3
3	P-Q4	PxP
4	NxP	N-B3
5	N-QB3	P-K4!?
6	N/4-N5	P-Q3
7	P-QR4	P-QR3
8	N-R3	B-K3
9	B-B4	BxB
10	NxB	NxP?[1]
11	NxN	P-Q4
12	B-N5	P-B3[2]
	see diagram	
13	BxP	PxB
14	QxP!	B-K2[3]
15	N/B-Q6†	BxN
16	NxB†	K-K2
17	O-O-O	N-Q5
18	RxN![4]	. . . .

WHITE TO PLAY

Though Black is a Piece down, his Pawns are attacking three White pieces. But, paradoxically, Black's Queen Pawn is vulnerable.

White has a winning attack

---

[1] A serious miscalculation which loses.

[2] Other moves are no better, e.g. 12 ... Q–Q2; 13 N–N6 or 12 ... B–K2 or 12 ... N–K2; 13 N(K4)–Q6†!, K–B1; 14 QxP! or 13 ... K–Q2; 14 NxBP.

[3] Naturally, if 14 ... QxQ; 15 NxP† and 16 NxQ wins easily.

[4] 18 ... PxR; 19 R–K1†, K–Q2; 20 NxP† and 21 NxQ, and Black has nothing left.

	WHITE	BLACK
1	P-K4	P-QB4
2	N-KB3	N-KB3
3	N-B3	P-Q4
4	PxP	NxP
5	P-Q4	P-K3[1]
6	NxN	QxN
7	B-K3	PxP
8	NxP	P-QR3
9	B-K2	QxNP
10	B-B3	Q-N3
11	Q-Q2	P-K4?[2]

see diagram

12	O-O-O!	PxN
13	BxQP	N-B3[3]
14	B-B6	QxB[4]
15	KR-K1†	B-K2[5]
16	BxN†	K-B1[6]
17	Q-Q8†	BxQ
18	R-K8	. . . .

**Black has been
checkmated**

WHITE TO PLAY

*Black has won a Pawn and
has gained a tempo by attacking a Knight. White's non-
chalant development is the
basis of a deep mating combination.*

---

[1] An easier game for Black is obtainable by 5 . . . NxN; 6 PxN, P-K3;
7 B-Q3, PxP; 8 PxP, B-N5†.

[2] Black is behind in development and must be careful about opening up
the game. First 11 . . . B-K2 and if 12 O-O-O, then 12 . . . P-K4
(13 KR-N1, Q-Q3) gives White more problems, though Black's position is still very difficult.

[3] Other moves are no better, e.g. 13 . . . B-K2; 14 KR-K1, B-K3; 15
BxQNP wins the Rook.

[4] The threat was 15 Q-Q8†, NxQ; 16 RxN mate.

[5] And if 15 . . . B-K3; 16 Q-Q7 is mate.

[6] If 16 . . . QxB or 16 . . . PxB; 17 Q-Q8 mate.

152   *Sicilian Defense*

	WHITE	BLACK
1	P-K4	P-QB4
2	N-KB3	N-KB3
3	N-B3	P-Q4[1]
4	PxP	NxP
5	B-N5†	B-Q2
	see diagram	
6	N-K5	NxN[2]
7	Q-B3	P-B3[3]
8	Q-R5†	P-N3
9	NxP	K-B2
10	N-K5†[4]	. . . .

Black's Queen will be lost

WHITE TO PLAY

This position seems placid enough. And now White violates theory on his next move by moving the same piece twice in the opening, with disastrous results . . . for Black!

---

[1] This premature opening up of the game creates immense difficulties. Preferable is either 3 . . . P-Q3 or 3 . . . N-B3.

[2] And this loses. Better is 6 . . . BxB; 7 Q-B3!, P-B3; 8 NxB, PxN; 9 QxN, QxQ; 10 N-B7†, K-Q2; 11 NxQ and though Black's King Pawns constitute a considerable liability in the endgame, he can put up some resistance.

[3] After 7 . . . Q-B2; 8 BxB†, NxB; 9 QxP†, K-Q1; 10 NxN, QxN; 11 QPxN, White should win fairly easily.

[4] 10 . . . K-N1; 11 Q-B7 mate; 10 . . . K-N2; 11 Q-B7†, K-R3; 12 PxN mate, and 10 . . . K-B3; 11 B-B4†, N-Q4 (or 11 . . . K-Q3; 12 N-B7† wins the Queen); 12 N-B7 and White wins either the Queen with 13 NxQ† or mates with 13 QxN.

Sicilian Defense

	WHITE	BLACK
1	P-K4	P-QB4
2	N-KB3	N-QB3
3	P-Q4	PxP
4	P-B3	PxP
5	NxP	P-Q3
6	B-QB4	P-K3
7	Q-K2	P-QR3
8	O-O	B-K2
9	R-Q1	Q-B2
10	B-B4	N-K4?[1]
11	BxN!	PxB

see diagram

12	B-N5†	PxB[2]
13	NxNP	Q-R4
14	QR-B1	P-B3[3]
15	R-B7!	Q-R5[4]
16	Q-Q3	P-QN3
17	P-QN3![5]	.... [6]

White has a winning attack

WHITE TO PLAY

This is a good example of the danger in store for an exposed Queen, subject to harassment by minor pieces.

---

[1] This plausible move is a mistake. Simply 10 . . . N–B3 is preferable.

[2] 12 . . . K–B1, though unappetizing, offers better chances of holding.

[3] Black is peculiarly helpless. If 14 . . . N–B3; 15 N–B7†, K–B1; 16 NxR, QxN; 17 Q–B4, B–Q2; 18 RxB, NxR; 19 Q–B8† and wins.

[4] To stop 16 Q–B4.

[5] A subtle move to enable the White Queen to administer a murderous check at K8.

[6] If 17 . . . QxRP; 18 Q–Q8†, K–B2; 19 N–Q6†, K–N3; 20 Q–K8†, K–R3; 21 N–B7†, etc.

Staunton Gambit

	WHITE	BLACK
1	P-Q4	P-KB4
2	P-K4	PxP
3	N-QB3	N-KB3
4	B-KN5	P-QN3
5	P-B3	B-N2¹
6	PxP	NxP
7	NxN	BxN
8	N-B3	Q-B1
9	B-Q3	BxB
10	QxB	Q-R3
11	Q-K4	N-B3
12	P-Q5	N-R4
13	N-K5	P-Q3²
	see diagram	
14	N-B7³	KxN
15	R-B1†	K-K1⁴
16	RxB†	....⁵

White mates by force

WHITE TO PLAY

Black has too many weaknesses throughout his light-colored squares. White's exploitation of the situation is drastically instructive.

¹ 5 ... P-K6 is safer and gives equal chances. The text gives White excellent attacking possibilities.

² After this White wins brilliantly. Black's best chance was 13 ... N-N2 aiming for Q3. If 14 Q-B5, O-O-O; 15 N-B7, N-Q3 is playable.

³ Winning, for 14 ... R-KN1; 15 QxP, KxN; 16 R-B1† is lethal.

⁴ If 15 ... K-N1; 16 Q-K6 mate.

⁵ For if 16 ... RxR; 17 QxP mate, and if 16 ... KxR; 17 QxP†, K-N1; 18 Q-K6†, K-B1; 19 B-K7†, K-K1; 20 BxP†, K-Q1; 21 Q-K7†, K-B1; 22 QxP mate (or even 20 B-B6†, K-B1; 21 Q-K7†, K-N1; 22 QxP mate).

Three Knight's Game

	WHITE	BLACK
1	P-K4	P-K4
2	N-KB3	N-QB3
3	N-B3	B-B4?[1]
4	NxP	NxN[2]
5	P-Q4	BxP?[3]
6	QxB	Q-B3?[4]
	see diagram	
7	N-N5!	K-Q1[5]
8	Q-B5[6]	. . . .

Black will lose overwhelming material

WHITE TO PLAY

Black threatens to win White's Queen. White's next move will protect his Queen and pose threats which cannot be met.

---

[1] Very weak. 3 . . . N-B3 or 3 . . . B-N5 is better.

[2] 4 . . . BxP†; 5 KxB, NxN; 6 P-Q4 also gives White the advantage.

[3] 5 . . . B-Q3 is a little better.

[4] Black hopes to get in 7 . . . N-B6† winning White's Queen, but White strikes first.

[5] If 7 . . . P-B3; 8 N-Q6†, and now 8 . . . K-Q1 is met by 9 QxN, QxQ; 10 NxP† and 11 NxQ.

[6] The threats at KB8 and QB7 are too much for Black to handle.

156 Two Knight's Defense

	WHITE	BLACK
1	P-K4	P-K4
2	N-KB3	N-QB3
3	B-B4	N-B3
4	N-B3[1]	NxP[2]
5	NxN	P-Q4
6	B-Q3	PxN
7	BxP	N-K2[3]
	see diagram	
8	P-QB3[4]	P-KB4
9	B-B2	N-N3[5]

Black has wrested the initiative away from White

BLACK TO PLAY

White has played the opening carelessly. Black is ready for a paradoxical move that assures him a strong central front.

---

[1] This weak move allows Black to immediately seize the initiative. 4 N–N5, 4 P–Q4, or 4 P–Q3 are superior alternatives.

[2] A common pseudo-sacrifice which gives Black a free hand in the center. The sacrificed piece is recaptured directly.

[3] This move represents an improvement over 7 . . . B–KN5; 8 P–KR3, BxN; 9 QxB, Q–Q2; 10 BxN, PxB; 11 O–O, B–B4; 12 Q–KN3, P–B3; 13 P–Q3, O–O and the game is about even. However, 7 . . . B–Q3 also gives Black some chance to retain a minimal advantage.

[4] Certainly not 8 NxP, Q–Q5 winning a piece.

[5] Black has a fine position and an incipient attack with his strong Pawn center.

	WHITE	BLACK
1	P-K4	P-K4
2	N-KB3	N-QB3
3	B-B4	N-B3
4	N-N5	P-Q4
5	PxP	NxP[1]
6	P-Q4	PxP
7	O-O	B-K3
8	R-K1	Q-Q2
	see diagram	
9	NxBP![2]	KxN[3]
10	Q-B3†	K-N3[4]
11	RxB†	QxR
12	B-Q3†	. . . .

White mates next move

WHITE TO PLAY
So far, Black has hung on tenaciously--but White has a killer.

---

[1] The standard 5 . . . N–QR4 is to be preferred.
[2] Demolishing Black's King position.
[3] If 9 . . . QxN; 10 BxN recovers the piece and Black's position is in shambles.
[4] Or 10 . . . K–K1; 11 BxN. On 10 . . . K–N1; 11 RxB, QxR; 12 BxN is decisive.

	WHITE	BLACK
1	P-K4	P-K4
2	N-KB3	N-QB3
3	B-B4	N-B3
4	N-N5	P-Q4
5	PxP	N-Q5
6	P-Q6[1]	QxP
7	NxBP?[2]	....

see diagram

7	....	Q-B3
8	NxR[3]	QxP
9	R-B1[4]	Q-K5†
10	B-K2	N-B6

BLACK TO PLAY

*An old theme in new clothing.
White wins a Rook but loses
his King.*

**White has been
checkmated**

---

[1] Better is 6 P–B3.

[2] And this is a blunder which loses by force. White should play 7 BxP†, K–K2; 8 B–N3, NxB; 9 RPxN, P–KR3; 10 N–KB3, P–K5; 11 N–N1. Though Black has good compensation for the gambited Pawn, White has fair chances of defending.

[3] Or 8 P–Q3, QxP; 9 R–B1, N–B6†; 10 K–K2, B–KN5 winning the Queen. Comparatively best is 8 O–O, QxB; 9 NxR, NxP and Black should win easily.

[4] If 9 P–Q3, B–N5 is even stronger than 9 . . . QxR†.

	WHITE	BLACK
1	P-K4	P-K4
2	N-KB3	N-QB3
3	B-B4	N-B3
4	N-N5	P-Q4
5	PxP	N-Q5
6	P-QB3	P-N4
7	B-B1	NxP
8	PxN[1]	QxN
9	BxP†	K-Q1
10	Q-B3	B-N2
11	O-O	R-QN1
12	P-Q3	Q-N3
13	Q-N3[2]	PxP
14	N-R3?[3]	BxN
15	PxB	N-B6
16	QxQ[4]	RPxQ
17	B-QB4	N-K7†
18	K-R1	....

see diagram

| 18 | .... | K-K2![5] |

Black wins by force

BLACK TO PLAY

In this position, Black will win in the quickest way by deliberately moving his King so that his Knight may be trapped after 19 R–K1. But White's potential will be too late by far!

---

[1] 8 N–K4, N–K3 (or 8 . . . Q–R5; 9 N–N3, B–KN5; 10 P–B3, N–B4; 11 Q–K2 wins easily) ; 9 BxP†, B–Q2; 10 BxB†, QxB; 11 O–O, B–K2; 12 P–Q4 is a clearer way of setting off White's advantage.

[2] Black was threatening 13 . . . N–B5 or 13 . . . N–K6 winning.

[3] This blunder, which allows the Black Knight to cooperate in the King-side attack, loses by force. Better was 14 B–QB4, removing the Bishop from the Queen Knight file.

[4] Forced, as White was threatened with the loss of his Queen by 16 . . . N–K7† as well as the loss of his King Bishop. But now the King Rook file will cost White the game.

[5] Black threatens 19 . . . RxP† and 20 R–R1† and mate. Since White is unable to play 19 P–N3, and 19 P–R3 is met by 19 . . . RxP mate, the best White can do is offer a propitiatory piece sacrifice with 19 B–B4. But after 19 . . . NxB the attack continues with unabated fury.

160   *Two Knight's Defense*

	WHITE	BLACK
1	P-K4	P-K4
2	N-KB3	N-QB3
3	B-B4	N-B3
4	O-O	P-Q3
5	N-B3	B-N5
6	P-KR3	B-R4
7	P-Q3	N-Q5
8	P-KN4	NxNP?[1]
9	PxN	BxP
	see diagram	
10	NxP![2]	. . . .

WHITE TO PLAY

An old favorite in modern garb. Black thinks he'll recover the piece with material to boot, but is in for a dismal shock.

White retains superior material

---

[1] Though frequently good in analogous positions, here the sacrifice is unsound as White has a countersacrifice which carries the day. 8 . . . B-N3 or 8 . . . NxN† followed by 9 . . . B-N3 gives fair chances.

[2] White releases the pin and obtains a great advantage. Now if 10 . . . BxQ; 11 BxP†, K-K2 and White must choose between 12 N-Q5 mate or 12 B-N5 mate.

	WHITE	BLACK
1	P-K4	P-K4
2	N-KB3	N-QB3
3	B-B4	N-B3
4	N-N5	P-Q4
5	PxP	P-N4
6	B-B1	N-Q5
7	P-QB3	NxP
8	NxBP	KxN
9	PxN	PxP
10	BxP	B-QB4
11	Q-B3†	N-B3
12	QxR	R-K1†

see diagram

13	BxR†	QxB†
14	K-Q1	B-N5†
15	P-B3	QxQ
16	PxB	QxP
17	R-K1	P-Q6
18	N-B3[1]	Q-B6†
19	N-K2	N-K5![2]

**Black mates on the next
move**

BLACK TO PLAY
*White will be punished for
grabbing the Rook, and his
King will be strait-jacketed
by his own men.*

---

[1] What else against 18 . . . Q–B6† and mate?
[2] Black mates next. If 20 R–KB1, QxR mate, and 20 R–KN1 or 20
R–KR1, QxN mate. After all other moves, 20 . . . N–B7 is mate.

162   *Two Knight's Defense*

	WHITE	BLACK
1	P-K4	P-K4
2	N-KB3	N-QB3
3	B-B4	N-B3
4	P-Q4	PxP
5	P-K5	P-Q4
6	B-QN5	N-K5
7	NxP	B-QB4
8	B-K3	O-O
9	BxN	PxB
10	NxP¹	BxB
	see diagram	
11	O-O²	Q-Q2
12	QxP	QxQ
13	N-K7†	K-R1
14	NxQ	B-Q5
15	P-B3³	

Black retains his piece with a winning game

BLACK TO PLAY

White has won a Pawn, threatens to capture the Black Queen, and also threatens BxB. How can Black prevent disaster? Simply by allowing White to capture the Queen or not, as he chooses.

¹ More circumspect at this point is 10 O-O.

² Virtually forced, since 11 NxQ, BxP†; 19 K-K2 (or 12 K-B1, B-R3†!), B-N5† leaves White a piece behind, and 11 PxB, Q-R5†; 12 P-N3, NxP also wins for Black.

³ After 15 . . . B-N3 Black should win, as White's two extra Pawns are not sufficient compensation for the extra piece.

Two Knight's Defense

	WHITE	BLACK
1	P-K4	P-K4
2	N-KB3	N-QB3
3	B-B4	N-B3
4	N-N5	B-B4
5	NxBP[1]	BxP†
6	KxB[2]	NxP†
7	K-K3[3]	Q-K2
8	KxN[4]	Q-R5†
9	P-KN4[5]	P-Q4†
10	KxQP[6]	BxP
11	Q-B1	....

see diagram

11	....	B-B6†
12	QxB[7]	Q-Q5†
13	K-K6	Q-Q2

**White has been
checkmated**

BLACK TO PLAY

*Black is two pieces minus and
threatened with the loss of a
Rook. He wins, however, by
means of a coup initiated by
the sacrifice of still more material.*

---

[1] If White intends to capture at KB7 with the Knight, he should play
5 P-Q4 first. And if 5 . . . P-Q4; 6 BxP, NxB; 7 PxB, he stands
better.

[2] Black gets a tremendous attack after 6 K-B1, Q-K2; 7 NxR, P-Q4;
8 PxP, N-Q5; 9 P-B3, B-N5; 10 Q-R4†, N-Q2; 11 KxB, Q-R5†, or
here 8 B-K2, B-N3 and Black has a strong attack for the sacrificed
exchange.

[3] White has better chances of defending with 7 K-N1, Q-R5; 8 P-KN3,
NxNP, though Black has a fine attack.

[4] If 8 NxR, P-Q4! and Black threatens 9 . . . Q-N4† with a forced win.

[5] If 9 K-K3 or 9 K-B3, Q-B5† followed by 10 . . . QxB† and 11 . . .
QxN and Black is now a Pawn ahead with a winning edge.

[6] If 10 BxP, BxP; 11 Q-K1, B-B4† with a mating attack.

[7] Or 12 K-B5, Q-Q5†; 13 K-N5, Q-N3†; 14 K-R4, Q-N5 mate.

164   *Two Knight's Defense*

	WHITE	BLACK
1	P-K4	P-K4
2	N-KB3	N-QB3
3	B-B4	N-B3
4	N-N5	P-Q4
5	PxP	N-QR4
6	B-N5†	P-B3
7	PxP	PxP
8	Q-B3[1]	PxB?![2]
9	QxR	B-QB4
10	Q-B3[3]	B-N2
11	Q-K2	O-O
12	P-QB3[4]	P-KR3
13	N-B3	N-B5
14	P-QN4[5]	P-K5!
15	N-Q4	BxN
16	PxB	QxP
17	N-B3	N-K4
18	O-O	N-B6†
19	K-R1[6]	N-N5!
20	QxNP[7]	....

see diagram

20	....	QxBP!!
21	Q-K2[8]	Q-R5
22	PxN[9]	PxP

**White cannot avoid
checkmate**

BLACK TO PLAY

*White's win of the Exchange
has allowed Black a winning
initiative. White decides to attack Black's raking Bishops;
Black has a deadly counter.*

[1] An unusual move best answered by 8 ... Q–B2.
[2] A speculative exchange sacrifice offering fair chances.
[3] A better line for White is 10 O–O, O–O; 11 P–QN4, BxP; 12 N–B3 with good winning chances.
[4] 12 P–Q3 offers better defensive chances.
[5] Also if 14 P–Q3, P–K5!
[6] If 19 PxN, PxP and Black threatens 20 ... Q–N5† and 21 ... Q–N7 mate.
[7] Now if 20 PxN, PxP; 21 QxNP, Q–KB5 and mates at KR7.
[8] The threat was 21 ... Q–N8†; 22 RxQ, N–B7 mate.
[9] Or 22 P–R3, Q–N6 forces 23 PxN as in the text.
[10] The threat of 23 ... PxQ† is too much for White to handle.

Two Knight's Defense

	WHITE	BLACK
1	P-K4	P-K4
2	N-KB3	N-QB3
3	B-B4	N-B3
4	O-O[1]	NxP
5	R-K1?[2]	P-Q4
6	B-N3	B-QB4
7	P-Q4	NxQP
8	NxP	Q-B3
9	BxP[3]	. . . .

see diagram

9	. . . .	QxP†
10	K-R1	Q-N8†
11	KxQ[4]	N-K7†
12	K-B1[5]	N/7-N6†
13	PxN	NxP

White has been checkmated

BLACK TO PLAY

The threats for both sides seem to balance out, but Black strikes first with a six-move mating combination.

[1] Weak. 4 P–Q4, 4 N–N5, 4 P–Q3, and N–B3 are superior alternatives.
[2] Here White should play 5 B–Q5 and 6 BxN and 7 NxP with approximate equality.
[3] 9 N–Q3 is not much better, e.g. 9 N–Q3, NxB; 10 RPxN, BxP†; 11 NxB, QxN†; 12 K–R1, B–KN5!
[4] Of course if 11 RxQ, N–B7 mates.
[5] Again, if 12 K–R1, N–B7 is mate.

	WHITE	BLACK
1	P-K4	P-K4
2	N-KB3	N-QB3
3	B-B4	N-B3
4	P-Q4	PxP
5	O-O	B-B4
6	P-K5	N-KN5[1]
7	P-KR3[2]	KNxKP
8	NxN	NxN
9	R-K1	P-Q3
10	P-B4	P-Q6†
11	K-R2[3]	Q-R5
12	PxN[4]	PxBP
13	PxP†	B-K3
14	RxB†[5]	PxR
15	P-Q7†	K-K2
16	QxP	B-Q3†

see diagram

BLACK TO PLAY

White is a Piece ahead and has a passed Pawn on the seventh rank, but the weakness of the dark-colored squares on the King-side destroys him.

Black has a winning attack

[1] Customary in this position is 6 . . . P–Q4, but the text is not bad and it is tricky.

[2] This is inferior. White should play either 7 R–K1 or 7 B–B4.

[3] Or 11 B–K3, NxB; 12 BxB†, B–K3; 13 P–B5, O–O and Black has the better chances.

[4] If 12 BxP, B–B7!; 13 R–K2 or R–B1, BxP!; 14 PxB, Q–N6†; 15 K–R1, QxP mate.

[5] Otherwise the Rook at K1 will be lost.

Two Knight's Defense

	WHITE	BLACK
1	P-K4	P-K4
2	N-KB3	N-QB3
3	B-B4	N-B3
4	O-O	B-B4[1]
5	P-Q3	P-Q3
6	B-KN5[2]	B-K3
7	B-N3	Q-Q2
8	BxN[3]	PxB
9	N-R4	B-KN5
10	Q-Q2	O-O-O
11	K-R1	B-R4
12	P-KB4	Q-N5
13	P-N3	KR-N1
14	Q-N2[4]	....

see diagram

14	....	QxN
15	PxQ	RxQ
16	KxR[5]	R-N1†

**White cannot avoid
checkmate**

BLACK TO PLAY

*White's last move was made
to prevent 14 . . . QxN 15
PxQ, B-B6† 16 RxB, R-N8.
But Black will not be swerved.*

---

[1] 4 . . . NxP is the most effective means of exploiting White's careless sequence of moves. If White merely wishes to play P-Q3 he should do so at his fourth move rather than his fifth, avoiding this possibility.

[2] Since Black has not castled on the King side this is weak, as after an eventual BxN the open Knight file can be used for the attack. 6 B-K3 is preferable.

[3] Bad; White should not open the Knight file.

[4] This loses by force. Black was threatening 14 . . . QxN; 15 PxQ, B-B6†; 16 RxB, R-N8 mate, but White should try 14 N-B3, when his Queen Rook aids in the defense.

[5] 16 . . . R-N1†; 17 K-R3 (17 K-R1, B-B6†; 18 RxB, R-N8 mate), B-N5†; 18 K-N2 (or 18 K-N3, B-K7†; 19 K-R3, BxR mate), B-K7†; 19 K-R1 (19 K-R3, BxR mate) 19 . . . B-B6†; 20 RxB, R-N8 mate.

168

Vienna Game

	WHITE	BLACK
1	P-K4	P-K4
2	N-QB3	N-KB3
3	P-B4	P-Q4
4	PxKP	NxP
5	Q-B3	N-QB3
6	NxN[1]	N-Q5
7	Q-B4	PxN
8	B-B4[2]	B-KB4
9	P-B3[3]	P-KN4
10	BxP†[4]	KxB
11	Q-B2[5]	....

see diagram

11	....	P-K6!
12	Q-B1	PxP†
13	K-Q1[6]	PxB/Q†
14	KxQ	P-N5
15	P-N4[7]	Q-N4†
16	K-Q1	R-Q1

Black has a winning attack

BLACK TO PLAY

White is confident that if Black proceeds 11 ... N-B7† 12 K-Q1, NxR, then 13 QxB wins. So far White's reasoning is correct; but Black has a devastating answer.

[1] Better is 6 B–N5. The text move loses valuable time.
[2] If 8 QxP, B–KB4 and 9 ... NxP† wins.
[3] Better 9 B–N3, but White has a terrible position.
[4] The Queen has no good moves to attack the Bishop. If 10 Q–B2, P–K6!; 11 PxP, N–B7†; 12 K–K2, B–N5†; 13 K–B1 (13 N–B3, NxR), Q–Q8†; or 10 Q–B1, N–B7†; 11 K–K2 (11 K–Q1, N–K6†), B–N5†.
[5] Again if 11 Q–B1, N–B7†; 12 K–K2 (12 K–Q1, N–K6† or 12 K–B2, NxR), Q–Q6† wins.
[6] On 13 BxP, N–B7† or 13 KxP, N–B7†, the rest is mayhem.
[7] If 15 PxN, B–R3†; 16 K–Q1, QxP†; 17 K–K1, Q–Q7 mate.

Vienna Game

	WHITE	BLACK
1	P-K4	P-K4
2	N-QB3	N-KB3
3	P-B4	P-Q4
4	BPxP	NxP
5	N-B3	B-KN5
6	Q-K2	N-B4[1]
7	P-Q4	BxN?[2]
8	QxB	Q-R5†
9	P-N3	QxQP
10	B-K3!	QxP
11	O-O-O	P-QB3

see diagram

	WHITE	BLACK
12	NxP!	PxN
13	RxP	Q-K3?[3]
14	B-QB4	Q-K5[4]
15	BxN	. . . .[5]

White has a winning attack

WHITE TO PLAY

Black's Queen has consumed a lot of time on a Pawn-hunting safari. Her neglected consort will soon be without resource. 15 . . . QxQ is irrelevant.

---

[1] 6 . . . N-N4; 7 P-KR4, NxN†; 8 PxN, B-K3; 9 P-Q4, N-B3; 10 B-K3, B-K2; 11 Q-B2, Q-Q2 followed by 12 . . . O-O-O is a more reasonable way of playing for Black.

[2] And this capture in order to gain Pawns is decidedly risky. 7 . . . N-K3 was greatly to be preferred.

[3] Immediately 13 . . . Q-K5, allowing White to regain the piece by 14 QxQ, NxQ; 15 R-K5† offered slim chances of holding, but was much better than the text.

[4] For White threatened 15 RxN or 15 R-Q8†.

[5] If 15 . . . QxQ; 16 R-K1†, B-K2; 17 RxB†, K-B1; 18 R-Q8 mate.

170

	WHITE	BLACK
1	P-K4	P-K4
2	N-QB3	N-KB3
3	P-B4	P-Q4
4	PxKP	NxP
5	N-B3	B-KN5
6	Q-K2	N-QB3?[1]
7	NxN	N-Q5
8	Q-Q3!	BxN
	see diagram	
9	N-B2[2]	. . . .

White wins material

WHITE TO PLAY

Black expects 9 PxB, PxN 10 QxP, Q-R5† 11 QxQ, NxKBP† etc., with the edge for Black. White's simple Knight move is overlooked.

---

[1] 6 . . . N-N4 is the right move. The text is the introduction to an unsound sacrifice.

[2] Or 9 N-N3. Black must lose a piece.

Vienna Game

	WHITE	BLACK
1	P-K4	P-K4
2	N-QB3	N-KB3
3	P-B4	P-Q4
4	BPxP	NxP
5	P-Q3	NxN
6	PxN	P-Q5
7	N-B3	P-QB4
8	B-K2	B-K2
9	O-O	O-O
10	Q-K1	P-B3
11	Q-N3	BPxP
12	B-R6	B-B3
13	NxKP![1]	PxP?[2]

see diagram

14	P-Q4!	B-K3[3]
15	RxB![4]	QxR
16	B-KN5	Q-B7†
17	QxQ	RxQ
18	KxR	PxP
19	B-B3[5]	....

White wins decisive material

WHITE TO PLAY

White has a winning continuation based on simultaneous attacks on the Black royal consort.

[1] A fine sacrifice which cannot be accepted because if 13 ... BxN; 14 QxB, PxB; 15 RxR†, QxR; 16 R-KB1, Q-Q1; 17 B-R5 wins.
[2] Black should not allow White's King Bishop possible activity on the QR2–KN8 diagonal. Better was 13 ... K-R1.
[3] Not 14 ... QxP†; 15 B-K3, QxN; 16 QxQ, BxQ; 17 B-B4†, etc.
[4] This exchange sacrifice wins, since 16 ... Q-B4? loses to 17 B-KN4!
[5] Black has no compensation for his piece minus.

172

Vienna Game

	WHITE	BLACK
1	P-K4	P-K4
2	N-QB3	N-KB3
3	P-B4	P-Q4
4	PxKP	NxP
5	P-Q3	B-QN5!¹
6	PxN²	....

see diagram

		BLACK
6	....	Q-R5†
7	K-K2³	PxP
8	Q-Q4⁴	B-N5†
9	N-B3	PxN†
10	K-K3	N-B3
11	B-N5	PxP
12	R-KN1	B-QR4
13	BxN†	PxB
14	Q-K4	B-N3†
15	K-Q3	O-O-O†⁵

**White will be checkmated
or lose his Queen**

BLACK TO PLAY

White's King and Queen, so dangerously exposed, will go down together. Simple development by Black makes for a speedy finish.

¹ 5 . . . NxN followed by 6 . . . P-Q5 also gives Black a good game, but not 5 . . . Q-R5†; 6 P-N3, NxP; 7 N-B3, Q-R4; 8 NxP, B-N5; 9 B-N2, NxR; 10 NxP†, K-Q2; 11 NxR with the superior position.

² Now, however, this capture is very risky.

³ If 7 K-Q2, P-Q5 and if 7 P-N3, QxKP†; 8 Q, B, or N-K2 (8 K-B2, B-B4†), QxR.

⁴ It is very awkward for White to meet the threat of 8 . . . B-N5† and develop effectively, e.g. 8 P-KR3 (hoping to sacrifice the exchange if 8 . . . B-N5†; 9 PxB), N-B3; 9 B-K3, B-K3 threatening the devastating check at QB5.

⁵ Now the fastest and most merciful finish after 16 K-B4 is achieved by 16 . . . R-Q5†; 17 QxR, B-K3†; 18 K-N4, QxQ†; 19 K-R3, B-B4†; 20 P-N4, QxP mate.

Vienna Game

	WHITE	BLACK
1	P-K4	P-K4
2	N-QB3	N-QB3
3	B-B4	B-B4
4	Q-N4!	Q-B3?[1]
5	N-Q5	QxP†
6	K-Q1	K-B1
7	N-R3	Q-Q5
8	P-Q3	B-N3[2]
9	R-B1	N-B3[3]
10	RxN	P-Q3[4]

see diagram

11	QxP†[5]	KxQ
12	B-R6†	K-N1
13	R-N6†	RPxR[6]
14	N-B6	. . . .

Black has been
checkmated

WHITE TO PLAY

*Black's hope to stem White's
attack by counter-attack on
the Queen is elegantly refuted.*

---

[1] This expedition loses too much time. Necessary was 4 . . . K–B1 or
4 . . . P–KN3.
[2] White was threatening to trap the Queen with 9 P–B3.
[3] Hoping to block the Bishop file and gain time for defense. White was
threatening 10 NxB, RPxN; 11 RxP†.
[4] Black had counted on this move to gain time by the attack on the
White Queen. Naturally if 10 . . . PxR; 11 B–R6† and 12 Q–N7 wins
directly.
[5] Forces mate brilliantly.
[6] Or 13 . . . BPxR; 14 N–B6 or 14 N–K7 mate.

	WHITE	BLACK
1	P-K4	P-K4
2	N-QB3	N-QB3
3	B-B4	B-B4
4	Q-N4	Q-B3
5	N-Q5	QxP†
6	K-Q1	K-B1
7	N-R3	Q-Q5
8	P-Q3	P-Q3
9	Q-R4	BxN
10	QxB	N-R4
11	R-KB1	NxB
12	Q-Q7	P-KB3¹

WHITE TO PLAY

How can White shatter Black's K-side Pawn barrier?

see diagram

13	NxKBP	Q-B7²
14	RxQ	BxR
15	N-R5	

White checkmates or wins material

¹ Now if 12 P–B3, NxP†; 13 BxN, Q–R5†, etc.
² The alternative 13 . . . PxN is also unsatisfactory, as can be seen from the following: 14 RxP†, NxR; 15 B–R6†, K–N1; 16 Q–N7 mate.

Vienna Game

175

	WHITE	BLACK
1	P-K4	P-K4
2	N-QB3	N-QB3
3	P-B4	B-B4
4	N-B3	P-Q3
5	P-B5	N-B3
6	P-KR3	P-Q4
7	NxKP	NxP
8	N-B3[1]	....

see diagram

8	....	Q-R5†[2]
9	NxQ	B-B7†
10	K-K2	N-Q5†
11	K-Q3	N-B4

**White has been
checkmated**

BLACK TO PLAY

*Apparently everything in
White's position holds, but
Black disillusions him with a
bolt from the blue!*

---

[1] White tries to stop ... Q–R5†.
[2] Black plays it, anyhow!

Index of Opening Gambits

Index of Opening Gambits
(cont.)

Index of First Moves

Index of First Moves
(cont.)

QUEEN'S PAWN

RESHEVSKY on
The Fischer-Spassky Games
by Samuel Reshevsky

The complete match! Authoritative, in-depth analysis of each exciting game by an International Grand Master and U.S. Chess Champion.

The World Championship chess match between Bobby Fischer and Boris Spassky has been called "the chess match of the century." Samuel Reshevsky, International Grandmaster and U.S. Chess Champion, followed each game, described the moves and commented on them for both *The New York Times* and T.V. Channel 5 in New York City. Here are all them moves from start to finish of this dramatic match — complete with diagrams and the expert analysis of a master who defeated both the Russian World Champion in 1952 and Fischer himself in 1960.

Samuel Reshevsky was born in Poland in 1911. He learned the moves of chess when he was four years old by watching his father play with his friends. He arrived in the U.S. in 1920 after touring European countries, displaying his skill, which included blindfold exhibitions.

In 1934, he became the U.S. chess champion, a title he won eight times. In 1935, he received the title of Grandmaster in Margate, England, where he won first prize in an International Tournament in which world champion, Raul Capablanca, participated, and defeated him in their individual encounter. Reshevsky has participated in many international competitions with commendable results.

In 1952, Reshevsky played board number one on a U.S. team against a Soviet team. He defeated Michael Botvinnik, world champion, $2\frac{1}{2}$ to $1\frac{1}{2}$.

In 1960, Reshevsky defeated Robert Fischer in a match. After 11 games the score was tied $5\frac{1}{2}$ to $5\frac{1}{2}$; Fischer refused to continue, and Reshevsky won the match by forfeit.

Reshevsky has written several books on chess. He also has written for newspapers and magazines, including the *New York Times* and the old *Herald Tribune*. **$1.45**